Michael

A Seven Year Journey Around the World

Discovering My Passion and Purpose

Ride that bike across china !

Julie Salisbury

Julie Ann Salisbury

IDistinctive Management Co.
Victoria, B.C. Canada

www.nomadaroundtheworld.com

Order this book online at www.trafford.com/08-0320
or email orders@trafford.com

Most Trafford titles are also available at major online book retailers.

Note for Librarians: A cataloguing record for this book is available from Library
and Archives Canada at www.collectionscanada.ca/amicus/index-e.html

Printed in Victoria, BC, Canada.

ISBN: 978-1-4251-7324-1

*We at Trafford believe that it is the responsibility of us all, as both individuals
and corporations, to make choices that are environmentally and socially sound.
You, in turn, are supporting this responsible conduct each time you purchase a
Trafford book, or make use of our publishing services. To find out how you are
helping, please visit www.trafford.com/responsiblepublishing.html*

*Our mission is to efficiently provide the world's finest, most comprehensive
book publishing service, enabling every author to experience success.
To find out how to publish your book, your way, and have it available
worldwide, visit us online at www.trafford.com/10510*

 www.trafford.com

North America & international
toll-free: 1 888 232 4444 (USA & Canada)
phone: 250 383 6864 • fax: 250 383 6804 • email: info@trafford.com

The United Kingdom & Europe
phone: +44 (0)1865 722 113 • local rate: 0845 230 9601
facsimile: +44 (0)1865 722 868 • email: info.uk@trafford.com

10 9 8 7 6 5 4 3 2 1

To:

My dear sister Tina
Who never faltered in her support and love for the crazy things I
did.

and to

My Mum who was mostly confused about my life decisions, but
still stuck by me.

and to

Greg, my dear husband, who always gives me unconditional love

and in memory of:

Bea

Who made me promise to write her letters every two weeks, and
then returned the letters to me four years later and told me to write
a book. I'm sorry she didn't get to see it.

"Stuff your eyes with wonder…live as if you'd drop dead in 10 seconds. See the world. It's more fantastic than any dream…..Ask no guarantees; ask for no security, there never was such an animal. And if there were, it would be related to the great sloth which hangs upside down in a tree, all day, everyday, sleeping its life away."

Fahrenheit 451. Ray Bradbury

About the Author

Born in Leicester, England, the middle of three daughters, Julie studied Business and Marketing at College and quickly moved upwards in her career in Product Marketing in the U.K. She succeeded early in her profession and enjoyed the international travel and perks that came with the job. When she decided to change her life in 1998 and travel around the world to live her dream, she eschewed all the traditional values of consumerism and learnt a different way of life.

She has visited over 35 countries and lived in South Africa, East Africa, Thailand, Malaysia, Mexico, Canada and of course, England. She has just become a permanent resident in Canada and lives in Victoria, B.C. with her Canadian husband Greg.

Publishing background

In April 2001, Julie visited family in the U.K. and was featured in the national newspaper, 'The Daily Mail' as the cover story for 'Femail Magazine' entitled 'Shirley Valentine 2001'.
www.femail.co.uk
You can read the cover story with this link:
http://www.dailymail.co.uk/pages/live/femail/article.html?in_article_id=41338&in_page_id=1879

As a result of the publicity from the cover story she was interviewed by Anglia TV on a chat show, Satellite TV series on 'Exceptional Women' and invited to many other regional TV interviews she was unable to attend because of her scheduled return to Thailand.

A 1500 word feature on "Sailing the Surin & Similan islands of Thailand" was published in March 2000 in the Sailing Central Magazine. This story can be read in full at
www.cruiser.net/khulula

Other travel stories and photographs of the journey on Seafire down the USA Pacific Coast, Baja California, the Sea of Cortez, Mexico and England can be read on
www.nomadaroundtheworld.com/adventure

Since residing in Victoria Julie has been featured on Shaw TV Daily show and has a regular radio segment on CFAX1070AM radio "Living with Passion" as well as other local radio stations.

Contents

"A Philosophic movement of the 18th Century marked by questioning of traditional doctrines and values, a tendency towards human individualism, and an emphasis on the idea of universal human progress, the empirical method in science, and the free use of reason" *Oxford English Dictionary*

Julie describes how she came to the decision to quit her job, leave her husband, all her possessions, family and friends.

"The minute you begin to do what you really want to do, it's really a different kind of life" *Buckminster Fuller"*

In Zululand the sailing yacht 'Khulula' becomes her new home.

"Life tends to respond to our outlook, to shape itself to meet our expectations" *Rich Devos*

Island tales include tiny islands off the coast of Africa, and the spice islands of Zanzibar and Pemba

"We all have the extraordinary coded within us, waiting to be released" *Jean Houston*

Once again facing her fears in dense fog and storms at sea she discovers the Pacific Coast is anything but 'a pacified ocean' The local fishermen and people of the West coast turn out to be charming and the prolific wildlife surprising.

"You must take your chance" *William Shakespeare*

Julie describes the scenery, the wildlife and the local Mexican fishermen in a way that brings it to life.

Acknowledgements

I first started writing this book when I lived with CJ for 5 days on the River Mekong in Vientiene, Lao. Several years later, CJ, an English teacher, was the first person to read my full manuscript, edit it and add her comments by email from Lao. She then proof read this 2nd edition when she visited Victoria this summer. Thank you CJ and good luck with your new sustainable hemp fibre farming project in Lao!

Big Thanks to my special friend Leanne Robinson (sister) who juggled editing my book and co-founding a non-profit with me to support a village in Cambodia subject to an illegal land grab. She spends 6 months each year in Cambodia and volunteers for licadho.org each year, going further into debt! Lee, you have the biggest heart I know.

Thank you Joan Christensen (and Dan) in Colorado, USA for all the time you spent helping me, keep sailing! Thanks also to Henri and Natasha van Bentum for introducing me to the Circumnavigators Club and bringing to my attention the fact I had actually circumnavigated (by accident).

Thank you Greg, the love of my life and dear husband for supporting and loving me and being my technical director, photographer and graphic designer.

Posthumous thanks to my dear neighbour Gail Burr-Tilley who stayed up all night reading my manuscript because she said she couldn't put it down! So sorry she didn't see it in print.

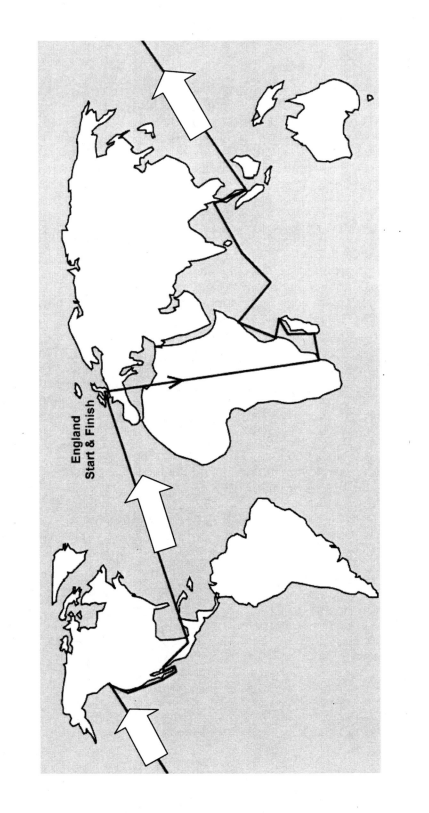

England
Start & Finish

Chapter One - Enlightenment

"A Philosophic movement of the 18th Century marked by questioning of traditional doctrines and values, a tendency towards human individualism, and an emphasis on the idea of universal human progress, the empirical method in science, and the free use of reason"
Oxford English Dictionary

I am the happiest I have ever been in my whole life. I have no debt, I live in a recreational vehicle resort, and I own nothing.

Eight years ago I was living in England in a beautiful 3 Bed Victorian House overlooking the golf course, earning $90,000 a year and driving a Mercedes Benz. I had an extraordinary career which involved travelling business class around the world and I was married to the 'perfect' husband. I felt deeply discontented with life and felt something really important was missing – I just didn't know what. That was the reason I started a 7 year journey around the World, to get where I am today. Not only did I complete a full circle of the globe, I feel like I have completed a full circle of my life.

It all started in 1998, 1 was 32 and I didn't want for anything. I spent my days rising at 7am driving to the office in my Mercedes for an hour, working for 10 hours a day and dashing home in time for Coronation Street on the TV and a microwave dinner. Following day, same, repeat until Saturday. Saturday go shopping and spend as much money as I wanted on whatever took my fancy. Sunday visit the golf club with my husband and friends. This seemed to be the life everyone was living so I really didn't understand why I was so un-happy and bored. After all, I had a great job with a great salary and perks. I thought it was maybe a mid-life crisis, but surely I was too young for that?

Graeme, my best friend of 12 years, had just returned from travelling for two years and I knew as soon as we got together, I could really open up to him and try and explain how I was feeling. I was really looking forward to seeing him; we always had great honest conversations and his absence made me realise how much I really had missed him.

"So, you got married whilst I was away? Sorry I missed the wedding". Out came all the photo's, followed by some real truths I realised I'd never discussed with anyone before.

"The thing is Graeme, I know John isn't exciting but he's 80% of what any woman would want from a good husband. He is caring, we talk non-stop and help each other constantly by off-loading all our problems with work. He isn't the greatest love and I always felt I came 4th in line to his work, his golf, and his child from his previous marriage, but it's a lot more than most people are lucky enough to find." I wondered who I was trying to convince.

"So what is it Julie? Time to change jobs again?" asked Graeme,"

"Well, yes, but I need to do something completely different; a new challenge. I need some excitement in my life".

"Well, I know what you mean; I now know exactly what I want from my life now that I've been travelling. I've come back to the U.K. to save enough money, and then I'm going to buy a yacht and sail around the world"

"A pipe dream Graeme?" I said with a smile on my face. He was always a dreamer. "But what the heck, sounds like a good plan. Can I come with you?"

I remember that conversation so well, because it was ironic. That was the kind of spontaneous thing I wanted to do with my life. People often say, "I don't know what I want, but I know what I don't want." Well, I knew, but I had far too much responsibility to have Graeme's freedom. He had no ties, no wife, no house, and no career or need to fit into society. He was a free agent and at the end of the day, he was my best friend, and I'd only just got married.

Despite all the odds against it, it all happened very fast following that first reunion. I wanted to see more of Graeme, but he had to find work, so I suggested he re-decorate my kitchen for a generous fee. John knew Graeme was my best friend, so he had no problem with him staying at our house for a couple of weeks. I'm sure he now regrets that decision because in the time that Graeme was staying at our house, I started to have fun again, and I fell in love with my best friend. By the time I'd realised what had happened, Graeme told me that he always loved me, but would never do anything to influence my feelings towards him. The feelings I had for him were completely overwhelming and I was being the ultimate bitch to my husband, but I simply couldn't help myself. To deny how I felt would be selling my soul. But to leave everything? I didn't think twice about it. I just knew it was the right thing to do. I suddenly had a whole new prospective on life and I knew John, my family and my friends would not understand why I had to throw away my 'perfect' marriage, house, job, possessions, and run away with a 'long-haired hippy' with no prospects.

John took it really bad, I tried to keep Graeme a secret because I thought it would make it worse, but in the end, it was the only way I could get him to understand what I was doing. How could he understand how I appeared to change so suddenly? He tried everything to win me back, and boy did that hurt, but I needed to go through that pain myself; to test my own beliefs in my new way of life. I never looked back and once Graeme and I decided that we were going to live our dream, life changed very quickly. All the things that were once so important; expensive clothes and make-up, possessions, eating out etc, meant nothing to me. For six months, Graeme and I did nothing except for work and save money. We moved into a tiny bed sit above a butcher's shop which had a miniature 2- ring camper stove, an old settee, a double bed and a view of the public car park. Graeme made bread and I took peanut butter sandwiches to work everyday, to save on the cost of pub meals or take-outs. We didn't have a television, and we didn't go out.

For the first time in my life I worked for one reason only: to make money! And I hated every moment of it. Now I had nothing in common with the other 'high-fliers' I worked with. I couldn't talk about films or television programmes. I'd sold all my designer clothes so I obviously didn't discuss the latest fashion or my spending sprees at Kookai. I sold all my gold jewellery, and once the Estee Lauder ran out, that was the end of that! Shunning normal society and protocol, I didn't fit in anymore. The only reason I stuck at it was a date I was clinging onto when we would fly to South Africa to look for our yacht and sail into the sunset with no expectations or accomplishments to comply to. One month after my devastating decision to leave my husband, beautiful home and great job to travel around the world, I looked back at my diary and read my own words, which actually sounded quite sane.

Diary excerpt 14th April 1998

Nearly a month later, it feels clearer already. I've been conditioned from birth, through childhood and adulthood for an 'expected' way of life. Parents endeavour to give their children 'the best' so in turn, we can also achieve to give our children 'the best'. Whatever the definition of 'best' is, it tends to mean material belongings. When you 'achieve' this, what do you do then? I did achieve everything expected of me but I made the mistake of thinking I was doing it for myself.

Suddenly I feel wise now that I've had the big responsible job, which comes with the immense car, big salary, and foreign travel and, of course, reverence and recognition. Now that I've lived in the large house with the nice garden, the 'social' friends of the same status and, to top it all, had the big white wedding, now I'm wise. I've suddenly realised I've achieved what Mum, Dad, relatives and 'friends' told me I was supposed to achieve. I suppose I felt special because I had 'over-achieved' until suddenly I realised I wasn't doing this for myself. I was so habituated to this way of life; I didn't even consider there was an alternative.

My friend Tanya is someone I always admired, she made the decision to look for another life travelling, and she's still doing it 4 years on. I still admire her but somewhere I think she may have gotten lost again. We always managed to meet, as she backpacked around the world, and I travelled for business. The first time I hadn't seen her for 12 months and I wrote to say I was due in Hong Kong in 3 weeks. We made a joke of it and said 'let's do lunch in Hong Kong' and we did! I will never forget the way she really appreciated staying the night in a business hotel and hopped off with the mini soaps and shampoo, and most of my wardrobe.

After that, we always tried to meet up when I did my trips to the Far East. We always had such a giggle shocking everyone in the bar with her backpacker clothes and hair! But then, when she left Hong Kong and I was due to go out again for the 3rd year, I thought, shit! Why do I want to sit on a plane for 12 hours, eat terrible food, live in a rabbit cage for three weeks, and visit hot slave-labour factories in China? I realised I didn't actually enjoy it that much but I thought it was cool to meet my best friend 'for

4

lunch' and 'brag' or tell people, 'oh, I'm leaving for Hong Kong on Friday', or 'did I tell you the time… blah blah'. As soon as I didn't have Tanya to meet there, it completely lost all of its appeal.

So I left the job (as I do, usually after two and half years, get bored and find a new challenge), and consciously went for one that meant I didn't have to go to New York or Detroit or Frankfurt or Amsterdam. Most importantly, I wouldn't have to visit the Far East for two weeks. My next round of trips was going to start again, and I had to get out before that.

I traded that job for one that didn't require international travel and paid an even bigger salary (seems most people consider international business travel a perk before you have to do it regularly…) But of course, that didn't help. I'd just traded in one type of travel for another; to sit on the M1 or M25 motorways, sit on trains and tubes and stay in different slightly larger concrete cells they fondly call 'hotels'. I was at a loss as to how I stop this sadistic cycle. I had no idea what the alternatives were.

Well, if you take down the shutters of 'convention' and expectations, you'd be very surprised. There's a whole world out there to be enjoyed; not to live to work, but to work to live, experience and enjoy. I always made excuses why I couldn't go travelling, like I was 'too small/not strong enough/couldn't cope without the luxuries in life/ need to work in order to have a challenge and achieve. Anyway, how could you find someone you're so comfortable with that could share it with you, rather than go alone?

I've also realised, perhaps without realising it, that I am a woman (strange as that sounds) with the needs of a woman. Man was historically a cave man, to hunt, protect and provide for the woman. A woman has a different set of skills to a man, like multi-tasking and nurturing, whereas men tend to focus on one task at a time (like hunting and protecting). Despite being the 'independent' woman, I've realised I need a man I can share this with. The reason I now say things are clearer is that I've found that man. The fact is I actually found him 12 years ago. I'm just a bit slow and I guess I needed to go through the process of accomplishment to understand that you really do have other choices in life.

So now I work for a different reason, to earn money! To save so I can now have the choice for an unconventional way of life. This does mean that the motorway travelling, selling and concrete hotel rooms are even harder to bear. The difference is it is now for a reason and I'm clinging onto a date six months down the line when we can cruise into the sunset.

Wow, when I read that now I think, 'wow girl, you were brave', but I also remember the incredible pain I caused my family and friends at the time. Seven years later I now realise that I had been raised, as we all are, as a magician, who observe and analyze then remembers things so that we can be graded. We then work hard and put in the time to 'prove' our knowledge, but mostly forget that our true purpose in life comes down to our relationships. We're too busy adapting our energy to fit into our traditional tribe, which in the first world mostly ignores the importance of community. Maybe it was my experience of learning the third world tribal ways that broke my vicious cycle. When you discover this, only then can you start to consider what would make your life more complete.

Diary excerpt 20th April 1998

Of course, to eschew traditional society means you will unavoidably cause a lot of hurt to those close to you who understand nothing other than this way. Family will not understand, but I hope they will eventually. Close friends do understand, but they are the easy ones. Why would a person who has succeeded within society, suddenly, in three weeks, want to throw it all away?

Parents who are from a different generation that have lived their whole life conservatively (and clearly remember the rationing that war caused) find it the hardest. They expect you to live up to their image of success, and don't really want to encourage you to grow as an individual; they want you to be what they couldn't be. I remember telling my parents I was going to the Far East on a business trip and was astonished by the reaction. I expected them to be 'delighted', not worried, because I thought I was living up to their expectations of success. Of course, once I came back in one piece without any deadly diseases, it was easier to accept in the second year. By the third year they were able to ask me in casual

6

conversation when my next trip was due, as though, now, it was a 'normal' way of life (and because their peers were impressed their daughter was going on such exotic business trips)

Leaving my husband was not so easy. Within the way of life I was leading, John was the perfect husband. He loved, he cared about my work, and we talked and helped each other with our careers, socialised with our work friends and lived in a wonderful dream house with a dream garden. Everyone now says 'you lucky girl, why throw all that away?' I can only simply answer that he was perfect for that way of life. Once careers, houses, possessions, colleagues to impress and cosy living are not important to you anymore, it is no longer perfect. The fact that our first wedding anniversary was only 3 weeks after I made the decision, made the pain even more difficult.

I was determined to make a new life work and it seemed that my new attitude to life was already causing dislike of the material world.

Diary excerpt 17th June 1998

I'm now getting very intolerant and really despise work. It's getting progressively more difficult to cope with the driving (my back has started to play up again), and the politics are insufferable. Graeme keeps saying 'Only 10 weeks to go'; and I know I really need to stick at it to make the last of the money we need. It would be so easy to avoid the 'horrible bit' but it really is the quickest way to make money. I now carry a picture of a Roberts 45 sailing yacht, and every time I'm tempted to tell them to 'stuff it', I look at the picture of the boat and remember why I'm doing it. It really isn't that much longer. It's a shorter time-scale than when I first started this diary!

We're really moving up a gear in the preparation. I now know the phonetic alphabet, which is used for radio transmissions to avoid misunderstandings. It's actually fun spelling out my name that way – Juliet, Uniform, Lima, India, Echo, and I try and use it whenever I can - even on the telephone at work when someone needs something spelling out! Graeme did his yachtsman theory last week and hopes to do the practical before we leave. I've become really confident about Aromatherapy and believe I can trade with it. I've made quite a few blends and treat all our own

7

ailments with oils now, and they work! I'm sure you need a natural feel for it and I really enjoy doing it. I'd like to get a professional diploma for practising but the ones available seem very superficial and expensive. For now, I might wait until we get to South Africa and see if I can get a correspondence course to study.

I really can't wait for our new way of life. I'll probably end up having to leave behind the problems of my old life like the house, marriage affairs etc. I might regret it, but the only 'compromise' from John's point of view is to simply 'sign' everything over to his name, because I chose to leave. I don't like leaving business un-finished, because Mum and Dad will probably end up with it, but at the moment there seems to be no alternative. I saw a solicitor who advised me to just sit tight because I'm in a position of strength. So I'm not trying to let it bother me too much. My happiest moments are evenings (I travel back home now to be with Graeme everyday from Chester which is a 4 hour round trip) and weekends. Days are miserable but they do have a purpose. (Remember!)

Diary excerpt 17th July 1998

See! Doesn't time go fast! Only six weeks to go at work (and three days but I won't count them) I've been thinking a lot about sticking my finger up at them. It's such a shame I can't hand in my notice at the end of July. I can't risk working my month's notice because I just know they'll make me go to Chester everyday and that'll cost £600 (approx $1300 CAD) in petrol at my own expense. I know the shit will really hit the fan when I leave at the end of August and never go back!

I'm seeing John on Thursday to sign over the house to him, I felt uncomfortable leaving unfinished business. He is going to sign over the endowment which I can cash in for £2,000(approx $4,600 CAD) (so that's my total settlement for 8 years together.) We're up to £24,500 (approx $56,000 CAD)now in savings, so with July salary of £2000 and another £2000 from the savings account when the notice is served, and the £2000 from the endowment, we'll be up to £30,500 (approx $70,000 CAD) eight weeks in front of target!

So we could have gone earlier, but Bea needs us here until the third week in September because Dick and Barbara are on

8

holidays and she needs emergency contact in case she has a medical emergency. Bea is 92 years old, and Graeme's Nan, and lives alone so she needs a family member she can contact. We have been telling her all about our plans and she is very excited for us and completely supportive and encouraging. She even gave us a money gift to help us along which was extremely generous of her.

I have been so surprised how quickly I was able to save money when it is not being wasted on rent or mortgage, fashion or dining out. Most of the savings came directly from my salary and Graeme paid for the daily expenses of food and rent from his casual work. It is incredible that you can save for a new life in just 6 months if you really make a commitment. Although it is still difficult to imagine pictures in my mind of what my new life will be, it feels so much more real now. I can't picture it because I've never experienced any of the things I'm going to see and do, so how exciting is that? I feel so comfortable with Graeme that it's almost scary. I feel sometimes that I lean on him so heavily. He is my whole life and I miss him so much when he's not around. I hate sharing him. He's mine and other company seems so boring compared to the fun we have. Which is a good thing seeing as we are going to be living in a very small space 24/7!

The stress took its toll on me and my historically bad back. I have scoliosis (curvature of the spine) and had major back surgery at 18 to straighten my spine, leaving me with a 10" metal rod in my back and weak muscles which easily spasm. I'd always had problems with it, particularly when I did long car journeys or became stressed. It was agreed before I took the job I was presently doing, that I could telecommunicate from my Midlands base which was ideal for my customers who stretched to the North, South, and West, and not travel everyday to the Chester Head Office, which was a four hour round trip. Unfortunately, as with many companies in the UK, the style of management tends to be very paternalistic and if you don't report in everyday to the office, they do not trust you to manage your own time. This left a bad taste in my mouth and was the root of all my back problems. Eventually my problem was solved by a particularly bad spasm which left me bed ridden.

Diary excerpt 14th September 1998

Wow! Time really does go fast – I'm here! As it turned out my time left at work was spent mostly on the sick and taking accrued holiday days. I hardly worked at all in August and up until we left I was off for three weeks solid sick leave (in bed). I was beginning to get really worried that I wasn't going to heal this time. I really had pushed myself too far but it's all in the past now. I went through the usual panic attacks about handing my notice in, and in the end I sent a letter in (Graeme wrote a stinker for me). Anyway, it was hassle free and I got my month notice paid in return for a five hour hand-over. You know the best thing? Here I am now in Durban, South Africa, the sun is shining, the pool is cool, the beer is cheap, AND I'M STILL GETTING PAID!!

And so, on the 14th September 1998, we boarded that plane. Mum and Dad were confounded watching their successful daughter standing at the bus-stop with just a back-pack that held all my possessions. My younger sister wouldn't talk to me and most of my friends couldn't believe I was really doing it. My older sister, Tina, was the only one who truly supported me and told me to 'just go for it'. She'd also chosen a more un-conventional way to live, now a landlady of a local pub.

Diary excerpt 19th September 1998

We've been here a week now and it seems that life just continues, strangely the same, but in a different country. Life is very much laid back and we've already viewed about fifteen boats, two of which look like they have great potential. I'm getting really excited about doing up our boat, but I already feel impatient. We've got a lot more to look at before we make a final short-list. It seems so easy to just 'chill' where you land and without some discipline you could just stay in one place spending money. We're moving soon. I feel like I need to see more and we've done very little really. I wasn't very impressed with Pretoria (a city close to Johannesburg), other than the impressive houses and spaces occupied by the whites in the suburbs. I was expecting a colourful scene of Africa and the promise of Jacaranda trees, but spring was too early and the trees were quite barren.

Diary excerpt 24th September 1998

Now I feel like we're experiencing the real Africa now that we're in Zululand. We're staying at Cuckoos Nest in Kwambunambi just north of Richards Bay. The countryside is breathtaking, surrounded by forest and the village is, as usual, very friendly. And of course, it is hot hot hot! We saw a great boat yesterday which we both fell in love with so we're going to make an offer and see what happens.

Of course, it wasn't quite that easy and after six weeks of visiting yachts for sale we found the perfect boat. We spent 6 months in Zululand working on our boat everyday getting her ready for cruising. A lot of hard work. We constantly had delays which prevented us from cruising, but we eventually left in May after re-launching the boat with her new name, "KHULULA", which means 'to be set free' in Zulu.

Launching Yacht Khulula, Richards Bay, Zululand, S.Africa

Impalme sugar cane fields, Zululand. Open air herbal bath.

Zulu festival of dance, Zululand.

Chapter 2 - A female nomad in South Africa

"The minute you begin to do what you really want to do, it's really a different kind of life."
Buckminster Fuller

Khulula – our new home

Waiting for the transaction to go through for the sailing yacht we had decided to purchase was a frustrating time. We had secured ourselves jobs at the hostel we were staying at, not only to distract ourselves, but so that we didn't have to continue spending our cruising budget on food and accommodation. We ended up managing the hostel for several weeks while the owners visited Cape Town, so when the final sale was completed on the boat, we still couldn't move aboard because of our commitments. Fortunately, working at a hostel meant we were able to accompany the Managers on the 'tours' to Umfolozi and Hluhluwe Game parks and the traditional Zulu villages, to learn the ropes so Graeme could take tours himself and I could 'sell' them to the tourists.

Umfolozi and Hluhluwe parks are side by side and just over an hour's drive from Richards Bay where our boat was moored. Hluhluwe is the best known of all the Zulu Natal reserves and it surrounds a deep valley formed by the Hluhluwe River. The park is abundant with Impala, Kudu and Grey striped Nyala, all very distinctive and different deer-like animals. Large herds of Wildebeest (a kind of antelope) are easily spotted and mischievous Baboons are often seen blocking the road as they stop to casually masturbate!

Umfolozi is an undulating wilderness of 47,000 hectares between the white and black Umfolozi Rivers. It is famous for the programme which saved the white rhinoceros which became endangered following an increase in hunting to satisfy Far East demand for the horn, which is reputed to have aphrodisiac qualities. The park now aims to keep a maximum of 1,000 animals and surplus is made available to other parks. This means your chances of seeing both black and white rhino in the park are extremely good! Many people confuse black and white rhino because it actually has nothing to do with colour. The white

13

rhino's name derived from the Afrikaans word 'wyd' which actually refers to the 'wide' mouth and the distinctive big square lips that the white rhino uses for grazing. It is the 2nd largest land mammal and can weigh over 5 tons. The black rhino has pointed prehensile lips used for plucking leaves.

Diary excerpt:

"Then on Tuesday we went to the park and I experienced my first wild animals. We followed 3 male elephants and watched them wrap their trunks around each other and wrestle – at one point 3 trunks all entwined in each other. You could see they were contented big soft animals that would only harm you if something really annoyed them – then they would show it by standing in your path and seemingly growing in size by flapping their huge ears to warn you (like they did to some tourists blocking their path with their cars.)

We saw lots of giraffes, many really close, and they just struck me as being exceedingly graceful and very feminine in every movement. The zebra didn't hold the same allure but the baby we saw did, it must have only been a couple of days old because it appeared uneasy on its feet and its fur was still downy. The rhinos with their fierce looking horns seemed more occupied with eating grass than anything else, but their thick skin looked like an old man's, even the youngest looked ancient! Oh, and the blue-balled monkeys that we saw were amazing, a whole family with the male dominant showing his incredible neon blue balls! All in all, quite a few days of new experiences with the promise of many more to come!"

3rd October 1998

I'm sitting on deck while Graeme and the mechanic are still trying to start the engine. As the sun goes down I was hoping for a glimpse of my first African Sunset across the water, but alas the low cloud will probably steal that from me. I love the sounds of Africa, the singing frogs and birds in an orchestral performance. I love the fact you can see the moon in the day, and at night, the tropical storms with the lashing rain, loud thunder, and the sky lighting up. The lightning is amazing to watch because the strikes change direction, one minute they flash vertically down and then the next flash horizontally – an awesome sight! I love the open *trucks that carry the forestry workers, all the women dressed in layers of colour, tightly packed together smiling and singing. It is amazing to see the road workers that empty out single bags of cement to lay a road by hand, labour being cheaper than machinery. I watched 20 or 30 workers planting individual turf pieces to replace the verge, all bent over carefully laying each piece. I hate the banks and anything commercial, it would be a really frustrating place to work because everyone is so disorganised and unprofessional and everything takes so long!*

7ᵗʰ October 1998

The day eventually came when we could take the boat out for the first time in the bay and I stood on the bowsprit and looked back at the boat in the water and watched her on the water, and took a deep breath, to inhale my new life. It felt really 'right' and I just knew I was going to like this lifestyle!

So, while we were waiting for payments to go through, we continued to work at the hostel and became temporary managers so Karen and Sean could take a trip to Cape Town. When they returned we rewarded ourselves with a mini holiday to Impalme, which is basically in the middle of sugar cane fields. We stayed in a traditional hut which is a large dome-shaped dwelling with a tiny door and window, a thatched roof and a dirt floor, but very cool and quite comfortable. We opted to have an open-air herbal bath, a speciality of the hosts who have their own herb garden and heat a large cast-iron Victorian tub using coals. We sat in the bath under the stars, topping up the hot water from the huge cauldron which was heated by the coals. A rather unique experience.

The Zulu festival of dance

That weekend was a special traditional Zulu festival and we were afforded the honour of being invited as guests to attend the festival on holy ground in the sugar cane fields and observe the performance. There was an awe-inspiring atmosphere, 600 dancers who were driving out the evil spirits in a mesmerizing beat, with worshippers in white gowns sitting on the ground on prayer mats. Apparently, this festival only happens once a year and they dance continuously from 10 a.m. to 10 p.m. and are privileged to dance only if they can afford the traditional costume (about $500). This can take years to collect and an interesting

15

part of the festival was to visit the many traders who had set up stalls to sell individual parts of each costume. Each year the dancer will buy a spear or an animal skin or headdress, until his costume is complete.

The dancers were grouped according to sex and status and each group danced separately forming a block of identical costumes 100 or stronger. The married men wore elaborate animal skins draped across their shoulders, magnificent feather headdresses, and tiny skins hugged their hips, exposing their taut buttocks. Their Zulu spears were thrown in the air and stomped into the ground in a rhythmic beat representing the Warriors, dancing and swirling to the rhythm of the drums. The maidens (unmarried) were young vivacious teenagers bearing their beautiful naked breasts anointed with oils and perfumes and decorated with elaborate Zulu tribal beads. Their striking beaded skirts swung to the beat of the drums, exposing their nakedness beneath. The married women were considerably more conservative in long decorated black capes, tall beaded hats and bead decorations. The unmarried men wore kilts representing the Scottish army who fought in the Zulu war, although these costumes looked more like skirts, with white tunics, a green necktie and hard helmet hats. It made you wonder how the beautiful maidens would be attracted to these strangely dressed young suitors!

It was quite hypnotic to watch the different dances (each group danced separately with the warriors being the most animated to the drum beat), and we were permitted to watch with the spectators, who were very friendly towards us and enjoyed practicing their English. It was made very unique since this was a traditional festival which we were very lucky to attend, given that we were the only white people there, as guests of our hosts who had a special relationship with the local Zulu people.

This was to be our last 'overland' trip since our travels from now on would always be aboard Khulula and we moved aboard at the beginning of November, ready to start our new adventures!

Richards Bay, Zululand, was our base while we got the boat ready for cruising. The harbour was built in 1976 and is the largest coal terminal in the world. This never seemed to be too much of a problem until it rained and your deck would get filthy with the black rain from the coal dust. We often saw fierce storms in the bay when 'fronts' came through with winds gusting to 50 knots and waves coming over the docks. One particularly bad storm hit when we were in the club house. A sudden wind started and a huge dark cloud was formed as the wind picked up the coal dust from the terminal. As the cloud reached the marina the boats healed far over in their docks, the mooring lines screeching under the strain and unsecured dinghies flying through the air. Graeme rushed down the docks struggling against the wind and rain, looking like an old flicker movie as the strobe lights from the lightning lit him up. He had to jump on the boat and start the engine, driving the boat forward, to take the slack off the mooring lines, and to prevent the strong wind from blowing it onto the docks. Fortunately these storms were not that frequent, and usually predicted by the marine weather station. They certainly seemed to add to the beauty of Africa.

Diary excerpts

12th November 1998

Being on the boat is just great! I've never felt so 'home' proud! It was wonderful to start cleaning up (although 5 days later I'm looking at it a bit more suspiciously) I'm settling into boat life quite nicely, especially now we've got the stove working and can enjoy home cooking again!

5th December 1998

It's amazing how life just settles into a new routine, we do work on the boat nearly everyday, the sunny days somehow seem more productive because when the wind and rain come I miss being outside.

17th December 1998

Nearly Christmas! We went for our first sail yesterday and it felt really wonderful. It was a festival day and we took the boat out in the bay to watch the formula racing boats, from a great vantage point. I just kept looking at the 'little' people on the shore thinking they were looking at the yachts on the water and that we actually became part of the show. When we decided to go sailing I felt a bit apprehensive, but Graeme was in full control and when we had the main up and then unfurled the big geneo she looked really

17

striking in the water, healed over to the port-holes, simply exhilarating and magnificent! One of our guests said he couldn't find the adjective to describe it, and I quite agreed!

We spent Christmas and New Year back at the hostel, helping out and celebrating with our old friends, along with some new 'yachtie' friends we had invited along to join us. To celebrate the New Year we watched all the fireworks and a midnight spectacular (of red emergency flares that lit up the sky) from the deck of the boat. It was quite breathtaking and a great way to celebrate our first New Year on the boat. As the weeks and months passed we stepped up our work on the boat to get her ready for her first voyage.

31st March 1999

Time and money seem to go so fast. We're both really ready to go now. Originally end of March to Mid April was our target, but we're committed now until the end of April, only another four weeks! We still haven't finished painting, but the music system and all other electronics are now installed (GPS, VHF, LOG, Depth Sounder etc.) However, the batteries are not properly operational and we do not have a fridge freezer installed yet, I wonder if we will ever be ready?

22nd May 1999

We're cruising! At last!! We were waiting for money to arrive from the U.K. and we ended up cancelling the transaction and asking a friend to bring some with him when he came out to visit us. We took 4 crew with us for our first voyage to Madagascar, Chris from Germany, Fabrice, from France and a Swiss couple called Nanno and Nicholas. It was a welcome relief to have another female crew member! The first two crew ended up waiting on the boat for 9 days before we were ready to depart, so everyone was really ready to leave!

The First Days at sea enroute to Madagascar

The first day at sea was very lumpy, very little wind, so we motor-sailed a lot. The Dolphins were incredible, we saw them about 4 hours out to sea, about 20-30, and 5 or 6 swam right around the front of the boat, a breath-taking sight, watching them all jump in sequence and play in the bow wave of the boat. Our first sunset was so beautiful, all around vision (this was my first one from the sea). The night watch was not so great. The sea was very confused and we had to run the engine most of the time. It was cold and very dark and I didn't feel at all comfortable. I couldn't even hold a course straight enough, for long enough, to relieve Graeme! Of course, getting up at 1.00 a.m. and then again at 2.30 a.m. and up again at 5.30 a.m. will take some getting use to! I already have my first 2 sailing injuries, the cupboard fell open onto my head whilst I was asleep, giving me a lovely lump, and then I did something to my little toe, it feels so painful I wonder if I have broken it, but it's probably just badly bruised. So we're on our way sailing (at least now we are sailing).

25th May 1999

Fifth day sailing, today the sea has calmed down a bit and the wave lengths are longer, the sun is shining and again I am enjoying myself. The last couple of days I've felt like I've been in a washing machine, being thrown around like a dirty cloth! I've bashed my little toe again so it's now bandaged up and I'm hopping around (difficult on an angle all the time). I've got bumps on my bumps, on account of 5 or 6 heavy books depositing themselves on top of me whilst I was sleeping. I have a lovely black bruise on my hip when I did an impression of a flying fish as I attempted to exit the head (the toilet), and threw myself across the boat as it healed over, hitting my stomach directly into the fiddle rail of the opposite berth and smashing my hip. Last night I felt ill for the first time, probably because of the pink scrambled eggs that Fabrice decided to cook for everyone, not enough food for a main meal, leaving us all hungry and little seasick! Feeling apprehensive about the future, I want to be alone with Graeme, but feel concerned about just the 2 of us sailing this big boat when I don't feel self-assured on the helm or being left alone on a night watch (even 30 mins is a challenge right now). I have mixed feelings about crew, can't live without them, can't live with them, I'm sure things will take their course and we will see what the future brings. This wasn't quite what I expected.

27th May 1999

Arrived Tulear, Madagascar, on schedule, it was our 7th day at sea. It's not the greatest port and I was just so relieved to get the crew off the boat and walk on land again, it didn't seem to matter

19

that much. It seemed to take forever to get everyone organised, and much negotiation to organise 3 "Puss Puss" into town (hand drawn carriages with a Madagascan man running along the ground in bare feet pulling 2 adults along at a time). It felt like a school party, we kept waiting around to get everyone together, and then we would lose a couple, find them, wait for them and lose them again! We had to do the complicated immigration and port control check-in, notorious in Madagascar for all the different authorities you have to check in with in a certain order, in completely different parts of town, Port Captain, health inspector, customs and excise, immigration, port taxes, to name a few! By the time we returned to the boat, the sea had turned into a confused gaggle of waves, with a strong current against a stiff breeze, and a flat dinghy! We had no pump and no way to get back to the boat, so poor Graeme straddled the inflated tube and paddled against the tide slowly getting lower and lower in the water, to reach the boat and the pump! At one point we all lost sight of him, but then the anchor light came on and we knew he had made it back safely! He then had to row back to collect us once he had inflated all the tubes again (we had no outboard motor).*

Cruising Madagascar

We spent a few days at Tulear getting the crew off the boat and paper work sorted out, before we set off alone to start our adventures as a couple. All went wonderfully well until sunset approached, and then WHAM! The calm seas suddenly started to build with a swell and an increasing wind, which continued to increase. Graeme was enjoying this to start with, until he realised we were going to be caught short with no reefs in the huge main and no storm jib to assist in 'hoving to' (This is a method sailors use to 'park' the boat in bad weather by backing one sail against the other so the boat makes no forward motion). It was suddenly a mad rush and panic and I was being tossed around again like a rag in a washing machine, whilst trying to wrestle a dinner together in the galley and emptying the toilet which kept flooding, and picking up various articles which were flying around! I was not happy! I don't know what time it started to die down, but I was seriously tired and it was early in the morning.

I couldn't help much, I tried steering for half an hour whilst Graeme slept by my side in the cock-pit, but my shoulders and arms were getting seriously stiff. I think I got a good sleep around 3 a.m. till 7 a.m. by which time Graeme had got the boat nicely balanced and had lashed the steering wheel with a rope so it didn't need hand-steering. Joy of joy! Graeme has now been sleeping for 2 hours and I'm not going to wake him since that is all the sleep he has had all night, and I'm happily sitting in the cockpit with a gentle land breeze (wonder how long that will last?) I will insist on anchoring before dark, we should reach an anchorage in time; we both need a good night's sleep and a good meal, and a good sort-out downstairs. Lots of things have fallen everywhere and there is a big bowl of washing-up I couldn't face doing in those conditions. Greater things on the horizon?

The Barren Islands and a Mouse Lemur

Diary excerpt - *9th June 1999*

Following a really enjoyable cruise up the west coast of Madagascar, we arrived today at the 'Barren Islands'. Antiranavo is one of the Barren islands and really beautiful with bright white sand which made up for the lack of vegetation (hence the name Barren) We waited for the swell to subside, and ended up rowing to the beach at 4 p.m. with our fish that we'd caught on the way and the smoker to cook it in! It was so beautiful there, I actually suggested to Graeme that we should have brought the tent, watched the sun go down, and stayed the night. This would have probably been a good idea, since as soon as the sun went down, the surf started to build. (At this stage in our cruising, our dinghy was a deflated Zodiac with no floor and 2 home-made paddles made out of a packing case!!!!) It would have been too dangerous to return to the boat without a moon, so we sat it out until 1 a.m. - making fires with the drift wood and trying to get some sleep inside the dinghy!!! We had just got cosy in the dinghy when a mouse lemur jumped on Graemes shoulder - much to his surprise, my surprise and the lemur's surprise; (For those who do not know, a mouse lemur has a striking resemblance to a very large rat!!!!) Eventually we got back to the boat (very wet and exhausted) and decided to move on the next day, since the swell was getting worse.

A royal visit at the small fishing town of Maintriano

We headed for the next fishing town - Maintriano, located on the Northwest Coast of Madagascar, and quite cut-off from any other major town or city. We were hoping to stock up on some basic provisions and cigarettes at this remote location. Again, there was quite a swell, but we decided to just let the surf beach us - which it promptly did!! Once on the beach we saw a sight we were not expecting. Hidden from the sea, was a red lagoon, about 500m across and no bridge! This was a lagoon 'dried out' and consisted of thick red mud - which didn't look passable.

Excerpt from letter to Bea, 21st June 1999

...we then carried on our journey and 3 days later stopped at a most beautiful fishing village called Maintriano. It was the most welcoming place, everyone so very friendly and happy. We anchored about 300 metres off the beach and rowed ashore. I got completely soaked when the surf hit the dinghy, but fortunately I had packed my sarong so was able to change out of my wet clothes on the beach.

We were then faced with this large dried-out lagoon which we had to cross, which turned out to be thick red mud! Graeme led the way, following some previously laid foot prints, and promptly sank, right up to his knees! It really was quite comical, especially since he had to reach down right into the mud to remove his shoes, covering both arms full length and quite a bit of his stomach in sticky red mud! I was doubled with laughing and so were the locals, who were watching our antics! The locals led us safely across the lagoon and then to a local watering hole where we could wash off the red mud. By this time we already had a number of locals and children gathered around us laughing and smiling and greeting us, and it grew in size until we had quite a party leading us through the village to the chief's house. What a wonderfully beautiful place, everything so neat and tidy, each basic hut with a cleanly swept patch of dirt planted with flowers and bushes, and not a single piece of rubbish anywhere to be seen.

Even if we did have a camera, it would never had made it through the dinghy episode, so we have no photos of the village or it's people, except a very vivid one in our minds of well-kept beauty and one which radiated warmth and happiness from the people. We were invited into the home of a family (I think the chief), and given hot sweet coffee (served in a large bowl) and pastries (like doughnuts). Following much discussion in a mixture of French and Madagasy, with lots of arms, and a little English, the priest was sent for who could speak English (he was a French-Canadian missionary we later learnt). We were invited to stay for lunch, and a wonderful meal of coconut rice, Zebu (a cow with a large hump), and fresh fruit. They also asked us if we wanted a shower (maybe we smelt a little from our days at sea, but I think it was more a courtesy because they realised we had a shortage of fresh water on the boat), and so we took it in turns to use their outside shower and given a bar of soap and a towel to use. This was all very welcome to us since we had been eating out of tins and not had a fresh water shower for some time (we washed in salt-water). It was not the usual welcome you would expect completely foreign strangers to receive at a foreign port, so we felt really honoured. We were then given a complete tour of the town, including the local school and church, and much to our delight, the local bar where we were offered a refreshing cool beer!

Eventually, we told them we had to return to the boat because we were unsure of the sea conditions and we may be prevented from rowing back to the boat if the swell got much larger. They invited us to join them the next day, but unfortunately we returned to terrible sea conditions, making it an un-safe anchorage to stay at. With no means of communication, we could only wave at our new friends on the beach and call goodbye, leaving them wondering if they had done something wrong perhaps? I sincerely hope they realised our situation, which they probably did, since they are also fishermen and understand the sea.

As we approached the North end of Madagascar we arrived in an area called Nosey Be which is a popular cruising area for yachts with its many sheltered islands and Bays. Nosey is Madagascan for 'island' and Nosey Be was the largest island in this group, with Helville providing a good sized 'city' for provisioning, water and fuel. We always laughed at the name 'Helville' wondering how a city got such a name, but quite honestly it was always 'Hell' going there with the young boys at the harbour fighting over your dinghy to 'protect' it from theft. You would always smile nicely at one of the boys and choose him to guard your dinghy, but by the time you returned, a little war had ensued and a different boy was guarding it and expecting to be paid again!

SAKATIA, and RUSSIAN BAY are two beautiful places to visit. Sakatia is a laid back island with a small resort/diving centre in one corner, beautiful white sand and a large variety of fish to see when snorkelling. Russian Bay is renowned for the marine life in this natural 'harbour' 3/4 closed in by land - turtles, dolphins, manta rays everywhere, and of course, really great fishing - seems incredible in such a large bay that we were the only people there!!!!
KISSAMANI is a small island (more of a sand spit really) where we planned to meet Brian and Ann to celebrate her birthday. We had a bit of a yachtie party with other yachts we had met in Crater Bay - Norm and Kim, Genevieve and Pierre and a couple of South Africans we had not yet met. This was my first experience of the 'yachting' community, sharing food and drink on our private party island - and I liked it a lot!!!

Giant Land Tortoise on Nosey Momoka

NOSEY MOMOKA, was our next stop, after a sweet departure from Kissamani. I was really struck by the beauty of this island - steep thick jungle with a small clearing at the northern end where we found a small fishing village. We strolled through 'the village', if you could describe half a dozen straw huts, a water cistern and a communal fire for cooking, in such a way. There was one or maybe 2 families that lived here, mostly older people, living a simple happy life amongst the palm trees in Paradise. One thing that struck me - I think they actually realised how lucky they were, judging by the smiles and welcome they gave us. The following morning we spotted, what we took to be, two large boulders on the beach. We grabbed the binoculars to find to our amazement, two very large land tortoises, probably 100's of years old!!!! We dashed ashore and approached them, expecting them to dash back into their shells, and to our surprise, they actually behaved as though we were the curios.

Diary excerpt 29th June 1999, Nosey Momoka.

...they were so beautiful, quite happy for you to be very close to them and touch them, I was expecting their heads to disappear into their shells, but they were far too curious for that! We kept

getting closer and closer until I was on my hands and knees looking straight into the eyes of the tortoise and stroking his wrinkled little head. When four fishing pirogues arrived with supplies for the village, one of the locals came over to show us that you could tap them on the back of the shells and then stand on their backs for a ride! Well, I thought that was a bit cruel, but obviously the tortoise was quite used to living side by side with the locals on the island, which is why they were not shy of us. I wanted to take one back to the boat! (It wouldn't have even fitted in the dinghy).

ANDRANIRA BAY - What could beat a sight like that on Momoka? The hidden bay of Andranira is quite simply, stunning. You can not see the entrance from sea-ward, and the small entrance is not visible until you feel you are going to run straight into land (trust, trust that GPS). This is what adds to the beauty, completely enclosed by steep rainforest and cut-off from the world - at least that is what it felt like. We spent a couple of days here, on our own completely, using the last of our oranges to squeeze fresh orange juice, and cooking Potato and Tuna bake with the last of our provisions. Such a shame we had run out of cigs, rum, and fresh fruit and vegetables - we could have stayed there a much longer time. (I now look back and I am totally amazed as a non-smoker that I let cigarettes rule my life so much!)

Islands of the famous Lemurs

NOSEY KOMBA started our next round of exploring, following another trip back to Helville on Nosey Be to stock up! This island is famous for the black lemur, who has bright orange eyes and a large elaborate tail. The villagers keep a kind of 'sanctuary' for the lemur's at one end of the island, for the benefit of the tourist, of course!!!! However, if you visit here, once you see the tourist boats depart, you get to sit around and feed the lemur's your old bananas out of your hand. It is not really an 'enclosure' it's a place the lemur's visit to be fed by the tourists. Not exactly the same as seeing one in the wild - but we tried that first, we had no sightings at all (they were all in the feeding enclosure I suspect). The island has a nice feel to it, despite the influence of the daily tourists encouraging the locals to sell their wares, and it does have the advantage of a fresh water supply. We paid for a local to fill up our containers with fresh water and carry them to the dinghy, Graeme then rowed the containers back to the boat and the 'helper' lifted the heavy containers from the dinghy up to the deck of the boat. It took the whole day to ferry enough water to fill the 100 gallon tank on the boat, so we made sure we were very careful with our consumption of water. The only other way we could 'top up' the tanks was by collecting rain water, which there wasn't much of, at this time of year.

TANY KELY was our next stop, with a beautiful palm-fringed beach and a colourful reef close to the shore. A great place for snorkelling (but day-trippers do come here), with great visibility and a good variety of coral and huge shoals of multi-coloured fish. It was nice to have the option of snorkelling from your anchorage, climbing down to the water from your boat. This was really the first snorkelling I had done from the boat and so I was quite nervous to start with. It was going to take some time to be confident enough to snorkel alone, which would be necessary, since Graeme could not see anything without his glasses and did not have prescription goggles. It always amazed me that he spent so little time in the water, considering the sea was our life!

NOSEY IRANJA (otherwise known as Turtle island), has a large sand isthmus that connects it to the neighbouring island at low tide. It is a nice walk across to a perfect oasis, although signs of building could be seen on both sides. I suspect the turtles have already moved to Russian Bay, because we saw no sign at all of their presence. This was the first time I had experienced a sand spit and it highlighted the nature of the tides. I realised we would need to turn around and walk faster back to the boat, so that the spit was not covered over by the sea, now coming into the land very quickly!

Indeed the turn of the tide actually made rowing back to the boat quite difficult, and at one point, I was convinced the current was going to take us past the end of the island and we would be carried out to sea. It was necessary to paddle really hard against the current to keep the dinghy heading towards the boat!

Diary excerpt 17th July 1999, Helville, Madagascar.

The following day we headed back to Helville and felt a little sad that this marked the end of our visit to Madagascar. As luck had it, our crew member, Chris, who we were picking up there, had met a local Madagascan girl who he wanted to spend a little more time with. Lily was a sweet 19 year old, with strange coarse long hair, which I later discovered was a wig, which she thought made her look more European and sophisticated. Chris offered to pay us for food and lodgings to keep Lily for the next 3 days and visit a few more islands with him, which we readily agreed to.

For Lily it was an interesting experience and an opportunity to learn English, for us, it was an opportunity to spend more time with a Madagascan girl and understand her perspective on life. I eventually persuaded her to remove her wig (which Chris did not even realise was a wig although he had been sleeping with her for the last 3 days). It made her look so vulnerable, with her sweet heart-shaped face, beautifully framed by her much lovelier short dark hair. In reality, she didn't turn out to be quite so sweet, harassing poor Chris, who thought she was genuinely in love with him, and not a prostitute who demanded the 3 day rate from him. I'm not sure who I felt the most compassion for, Chris, because he really had fallen head over heals for the sweet Lily, or Lily, who just saw Chris as another paying guest. Well, we had a lovely time until it was time to drop Lily off, and that is when another side of her sweet personality started to show through, demanding huge sums of money that were way beyond the means of Chris. Chris eventually did pay her an amount he could afford, but with a broken heart.

The British Madagascan Consulate from South Africa.

MITSIO was our next call via a small island we spotted on the chart, called TSARA BAJINA. As we approached Tsara Bajina, we were quite surprised to see an orderly row of umbrella's on the beach, and what looked like a large thatched roof amongst the palm trees. This was the first example we had seen, of turning a beautiful island, into an exclusive holiday resort at $200 per night!!! It was very tastefully done, with obvious attention to nature conservation, and they were very welcoming to the 'scruffy' yachties! We 'bumped' into the Madagascan consulate and his wife (who was English but was based in Durban!) and invited them to join us on a cruise to Mitsio the following day. MITSIO is a really spectacular sight - the 'famous' rock formation called 'church organs' really lives up to its name. It is steep-too right up to the sheer face, so you can get the yacht pretty close and see individual 'pipes' formed by the Basalt - a real piece of artwork!!! There is a lovely anchorage in the nearby bay, nice snorkelling, white sand beach and local fishermen willing to trade a large Red Roman fish for two T-shirts!!!

So we had delayed our departure from the wonderful Madagascar for a few days, but it was now time to cross the ocean again to East Africa, calling on a few islands on the way.

Giant land Tortoise, Nosy Momoka, Madagascar.

Chapter Three - A female Nomad in East Africa

"Life tends to respond to our outlook, to shape itself to meet our expectations." Rich Devos

The great thing about cruising is that you can change your mind whenever you want. Once we left Madagascar our original plan was to visit Mayotte, but given the state of our finances, we decided that this was not a good idea, and decided to head for Aldabra. Of course, we changed our minds again a couple of days into the passage as the increasing swell was hitting us beam on and driving the first mate insane! (This constant thrashing of the waves onto the side of the boat builds up a side-ways momentum which means you are constantly thrown from one side of the boat to the other and makes sleeping, cooking, and reading almost impossible) So, we quickly consulted the chart and decided to head for Glorieuses. This is a small, French island only occupied 6 months of the year by a French policeman, 2 military men and a Meteorologist station.

When we arrived at Glorieuses we found a really beautiful island, but it was not a great anchorage and it didn't look possible to row to the beach. Once it was low tide it looked a lot more accessible and we said we would try and swim ashore. Chris got in first and thought he saw a shark (or a dolphin?), but anyway, that made us decide to not swim! We took the dinghy and Chris did some snorkelling over the coral and I did some hanging over the side of the dinghy. The coral was white and really stunning, with lots of different fish. We decided not to attempt to go any further because of the surf and returned to the boat. (The reef was between the boat and the shore so you would be in danger of bursting the dinghy on sharp coral or scraping yourself if a wave tipped the boat in the surf).

Within a few hours we received visitors at the boat in a large skiff, a French policeman, two military men and the weatherman! To start with they were very formal, demanding to see our passports and interrogating us about why we chose to stop at this island. Once we explained our innocent need for a night's rest and offered them some 'Khulula' spirit (which at the time was Madagascan rum), their mood quickly changed. They invited us ashore to visit their weather station and military headquarters and we readily accepted, jumping into their skiff which had two powerful outboard motors. The four strong men and Graeme and Chris still struggled with the boat in the surf and I was the only one that escaped without getting too wet.

We then jumped onto the back of a tractor they had waiting for us, for the 2 km ride across the island, through the thick interior of the jungle to their base. The interior of the island was really beautiful, thick palm trees which let the sun slice through, but providing shade for the sand road. When we arrived at the other side of the island, there was a clearing with the meteorology building and the officer's mess (and cold beers!!!!!!). We had the grand tour of the met building - quite fascinating to discover that they transmitted weather reports to London twice a day, and that so much technology was housed on such a small island. A quick tour of the officer's accommodation, and that was basically all there was on the island, apart from a really beautifully kept grave-yard of the original inhabitants. Each grave was bordered by clean white pebbles, and the same pebbles were used to represent the cross, in the centre of the grave. A small gravel path led to each grave, again with a border of clean white pebbles, I guess this is what the policemen and military men did all day.

When they returned us to the boat, and we thanked them for their hospitality, they said we were much nicer than the last people that visited them who demanded a tour of the Island and then had an argument with the policeman because they were not given permission to go ashore. This then escalated into an even larger argument when they demanded to know how much the Island would cost to buy! When the policeman demanded to know who this person thought they were, trying to buy French land, he announced that his name was that of a famous movie star (who I instantly recognised). Neither the policeman, military gents or met officer had ever heard of any of his films, or recognised that he was famous, so he was promptly asked to pull up the anchor (of his super-yacht) and leave French territory!!

We spent the evening there and left the following morning heading for Mafia island, changing our plans once again, when we realised it would probably be impossible to go ashore at Assumption or Aldabra islands. Probably the main reason we changed our mind was the large swell that was still hitting us on the beam and starting that rocking momentum going again, and driving me completely insane!

Mafia Island and the boy who ate a banana without peeling it

As it happened though, the same happened at Mafia Island and we could not go ashore again because of high winds, although we did receive a visitor from the island who paddled for several hours, against the wind, to check us out! It turned out the poor boy was a little mentally challenged, and we invited him aboard for a rest. In the meantime, the whole village had to send out a rescue party to come and collect him! He was very happy to be sitting aboard and kept pointing to things, which we assumed he wanted. There was obviously some problem because when we offered him a banana, he started to eat it as though he had never seen one before, peel and all. When the village men arrived at our boat to collect him they were making 'crazy' hand signs to us as a way of apology. We smiled and gave them a few gifts as gratitude for removing the boy from our boat who had happily settled in and was showing no signs of returning to the island!

We rested for 2 days and once the wind died a little, set off for Zanzibar on an overnight passage. However, the winds died completely and so we didn't make land-fall at Dar-es-Salam until the late afternoon of the following day. We did not want to arrive in Zanzibar at night-time, so we pulled into the bay for a short stop-over (to get our feet on earth and have a cold beer!) As Chris left the boat (he was on the boat as crew to mainland Africa only), his last words to us were 'you'll still be here in 8 weeks'. His prediction rang true when one event ran into another, almost too many to mention, but first the engine broke down and it took four weeks for the parts to arrive, the bill was so high we blew all our savings, and we had to find some way to make more money so we could continue cruising.

We met some ex-pats, who were all 'aid' workers, at a small store which had tables outside. They had christened this 'the corner bar', and it was right outside the bus stop for the 'Dala Dala' into the city of Dar es Salam. We made friends with many of them who got involved in helping us get our engine parts and helping us pay for them! Many were keen fishermen who paid a small fortune to go on fishing trips and so a deal was struck that they would 'contribute' to the parts in exchange for fishing trips to

Latham Island when the engine was working. We also planned to take them all on a 'booze cruise' so they were always keen to see us waiting at the bus stop to get the latest news on our boat repairs. We became 'locals' ourselves since every time we tried to get into the city we would be spotted at the bus stop and invited into the bar to be bought drinks.

We enjoyed our time there, especially the trips on the 'Dala Dala' to the city where we met many colourful locals, women, children, chickens and goats all squeezed into the small space of a crowded van with small windows, often the sliding doors left open to accommodate the men that hung out of doors.

We also spent some time with Alex (European descent) and Fansar (from Madagascar) and their little one, Tina, on the sailing yacht Ice. Alex had been a live aboard 'yachtie' for 3 generations, making little Tina a 4th generation kid, to be raised on a boat. He was quite a character, a grown man of 32 who acted like a teenager being exposed to the pleasures of a city for the first time in his life. He would come home excited, clutching a pair of Levi jeans he bought at one of the aid stalls or telling stories of the discos he loved to visit until the small hours of the morning. He was often seen paddling his surf board back to the boat at sunrise (his dinghy was stolen and so this was his only form of transport from the yacht for the whole family).

When we eventually left we planned an outing to the beach with the family and both yachts headed for a small island. Alex was always up to crazy games and he immediately rushed into the waves to play on his surf-board as we sat on the beach with Fansar and Tina. We watched him get tossed in the surf on the reef and watched in horror, as we saw him trying to get away from the sharp rocks, unable to do anything to help since he was so far away. Eventually Alex righted himself and started to paddle back to us, from quite a long way out. When he arrived back, blood was all over him and he casually spat a tooth out of his mouth onto the beach, as though it was no big deal! What a character, so typical of the many people we met during our travels.

Winning a local competition in Dar es Salam

Excerpt from letter to Bea:

..Through the friends we met we found someone who could fix our fridge/freezer, we've been without refrigeration since it stopped working 2 weeks after we left South Africa, we've got so used to not having it, but when you have guests who are paying, they do expect cold drinks at least! Lady luck shone on us again and we won a local photographic competition, quite by accident! A man with a camera took our photos whilst we were sitting in the 'corner bar', and we thought nothing of it, since he also gave us some promotional hats and pens. It turned out to be a competition by a cigarette company, and we happened to be smoking his brand of cigarettes at the bar!

We didn't think anything more of the incident until everyone we met told us that they had seen us in the national press and that we had won 100,000 shillings (about $200 US), so we rushed to the office to claim our prize! It doesn't sound much, but it was to us, and we treated ourselves to luxury foods like instant coffee, cheese and Worcester sauce! It is very expensive to shop in Dar es Salam (because the goods are imported especially for the aid workers who get paid big salaries), so you have to be careful what you buy, and instant coffee at $10 a jar had been crossed off our list for some time!

So we resumed repairs on the boat and we've now renovated the wooden sailing dingy we bought in South Africa just before we left. At the time it seemed it was destined never to float, but Graeme gave it his usual care and attention and now we feel like we have more freedom to go places we could never go before in our semi-inflatable rubber dinghy we had to row everywhere! It is so wonderful to have the freedom to sail in the dingy a long distance and we visit other yachts a lot more often now that distance is not a problem. We're so proud of our 'little yacht' and I call it 'my baby'.

Stoning for thieves still goes on

We take such care of the dinghy, but our worst fear is that it will be stolen and we always leave it tied up when we go into town. Theft

33

is a real problem here, despite the very tough sentence given to anyone who is caught. Graeme witnessed this when he visited the city one day and saw a live stoning of a man who had been accused of theft. He was shocked to see this kind of punishment still existed; thinking this kind of sentence belonged in medieval times. In the future, we were very careful not to shout 'thief' with this knowledge.

One day Graeme had visited the city alone and I was alone on the boat in the cockpit when I noticed our sailing dinghy being paddled away from the shore. My first reaction was that someone was moving it, or using it to reach their own boat anchored out, but then I realised it was being stolen. I didn't want to shout 'thief' because of the consequences, but at the same time, didn't want our one and only dinghy stolen! I reached for a wooden whistle that I bought from one of the Masai Mara and blew loud, standing on the deck pointing and waving my arms in the direction of the thieves. This got enough attention from the local fishermen to understand what was going on and they then started to shout at the young boys. The boys realised they had been caught in the act and changed direction, rowing the dinghy back to the dock. I was pleased to watch through the binoculars that they ensured the dinghy was well secured before they ran off!

I think they realised they had been given a chance and I realised our relationship with the local fishermen was good enough that they helped out. Only yesterday I had passed on a supply of pasta when I was going through my provisions and spotted a few weevils. The weevils are harmless but I couldn't afford to keep them on board since they would contaminate other food in storage before I had chance to eat up the pasta with the weevils. It seemed sensible to me to give this excess food to the fishermen for their families and they were very grateful. We hope to head for Zanzibar, Pemba and then Kenya next week, so I'll send you a postcard from each."

The East coast of Africa offers great sailing (good consistent winds), fishing, and regular sighting of large groups of dolphins. The amazing sailing pirogues perform acrobatics, which you think should be categorised as 'extreme sport', particularly as most sails seem to consist of roughly sewn rice sacks or even plastic bags!!! It is very unusual to see motors on any of these fishing vessels in this part of the world! I was always amazed to see the rough

34

wooden boats with their 'out-riggers' powered only by the hand-made sails. The crew would jump from the boat and balance on the out-rigger, like a wind-surfer, to catch the wind in the sails and give themselves more speed, whizzing past our sophisticated yacht (by comparison) and waving at us.

Mombassa - Mtwapa Creek

This is a beautiful anchorage on the Mtwapa River; well marked from the ocean, but easily mistaken if approached from the North (you sight the 2nd markings 1st which guides you straight across the reef). I tell this from experience as I nearly guided our yacht over the reef on our first entrance, because I mistook the markings. Once inside the creek, anchorage space is restricted, but easy access to the village compensates!!!

We found Mtwapa a delightful local village, with good fresh produce and friendly colourful Kenyans. The women dress in bright layers of clashing patterns and colours from head to toe, with 'matching' slings for the beautiful children they carry on their backs or hips. I used to love walking into the village to buy fresh vegetables and fruit from the market stalls and always delighted in watching the women carrying their purchases on their heads.

Despite being a lone white female amongst a sea of African faces, they were always very friendly, smiling when I bought my own plastic re-cycled bag to carry the groceries! I couldn't communicate with them, but lots of smiles and sign-language usually helped. I would just follow what the locals did, selecting the fruit and vegetables (most of which I recognised) and then waiting for the assistant to write down the total. I am quite sure they charged me more (prices were not advertised), but since this was the only local place I could buy fresh crops, I was happy to pay whatever price they chose to charge me!

The incredible thing about this village is that it had the very first internet café I ever saw. The fact that this African village was offering public internet access (even though it was slow and expensive) seemed such a disparity. Next to the internet café was a hair-dressers and I noticed that these women would spend a good amount of money on their hair, winding their afro frizz into elaborate corn rows and plaits at the expense of their groceries if necessary! Next to this shop was the government water tap where you would pay to fill your containers with fresh drinking water. There were many Masai Mara men eager to help us carry our 20 litre containers the 2 miles to the anchorage to fill up our water tank with fresh water. We negotiated with 2 young men a reasonable day wage for the task and it took them most of the day to deliver the water to our boat. We invited them aboard when the job was finished to share a cold beer, listen to Bob Marley music, and share our stories. We always loved the opportunity of this kind of interaction with the local's to learn more about their culture.

The 'Dala Dala' mini-bus to Mombassa

The over crowded 'Dala Dala' (mini-bus) into Mombassa is very cheap and a real culture experience. You're likely to be standing with your arms or legs draped around various body parts of other sweaty bodies, or if you are lucky enough to get a seat, provide a lap for someone else's child/chicken or shopping bag!!! It's all done with a big smile and 'habari" (Swahili greeting). I spent many happy days on the 'Dala Dala' and I always found it a great way to get to know the locals since you can be left waiting for as long as an hour before it decides to leave the bus stop. The 'Dala Dala' probably seats around 12 passengers, but it will never leave until it has at least twice this number of people inside and the same number dangling or balancing on the outside. Some people found this frustrating, but I always found it an enjoyable experience.

Back at the anchorage, Kenya Marine Land (under management from yachties on a break), has an excellent restaurant (great for a treat) and their own Masi Mara who always befriended the yachties. Whilst they dance for the tourists who visit the restaurant, they will smile and share a drink with the yachties and tell their stories of their lives back in the mountains. Most of them have come to Mombassa to dance or make crafts for the tourists so that they can save enough money to buy enough goats for the dowry for their bride. Some get caught in consumerism and end up spending their goat money on new sandals or walkmans!

Excerpt from letter to Bea 1st November 1999

"Now that we are in Kenya we have an address at our first port of call – Mtwapa Creek, Kikambala. We have been made very welcome here and it is a beautiful anchorage, very lush and green *with all the facilities we need including hot showers (what a treat!), fresh water to fill our tanks and do our laundry, diesel, and a very nice village about a mile walk with a good market. It also has a nice restaurant and bar, all the facilities provided free of charge on the assumption you will spend some money there (too expensive to eat but we do treat ourselves to the odd glass of red wine!). We intend to stay in Kenya a couple of months so we will spend the next few weeks checking out the other areas, Kilifi creek and Lamu islands."*

Whilst in the area of Mombassa, we didn't miss the ebony-carving community of 'Wengi' (phonetic spelling). You hear them shouting 'Wengi Wengi' at the Dala Dala station in Mombassa, so we just jumped on to check it out. A large rough 'courtyard' in the middle of the area is full of men and women of all ages 'whittling' away at elaborate Masai Mara statues, plaques and various animal carvings. The women carve delicate jewellery, spoons and letter openers, and the children are busy covering up any mistakes with 'kiwi' boot polish!!!!! (Buyers beware) You have to look close and carefully but you can haggle a good souvenir here. We bought a few carvings to hang on the wall of the boat, promising ourselves that we would start collecting souvenirs for ourselves and possible trading items for the future. Alex had told us how he bought carvings and jewellery from Africa and traded with them in other countries, so we thought this might be a good money-making idea. We considered that African items might be of interest to European tourists in Asia, which we were planning to visit next, or even a trip home to England might be an opportunity to sell (which I did actually do a few years later).

Zanzibar and Pemba

A great sail from Mombassa, Zanzibar is rich in culture and spices!!! We anchored right next to the 'night market' which is a hustle and bustle of locals and tourists devouring magnificent displays of freshly caught lobster, crab, fish and squid. We tried out their 'pizza' which is a cross between a kebab and a filled pancake - delicious!!! If you're addicted to good food, like we are, you could put a lot of weight on at less than a dollar a go! We washed it down with sugar cane juice extracted with something which looked more likely to mangle your laundry dry during wartimes!!!! Climbing up the old stone wharf steps to the market was always a challenge from the dinghy, slick with algae and

37

refuse. As with many markets that are set up alongside the water, it provides a convenient disposal area for old cooking fat and scraps, as well as the local urinal. Your approach needed care to ensure a large pot of hot oil wasn't about to be emptied into the sea or that a local vendor wasn't about to urinate directly into your dinghy! Often we would return to the dinghy and have to remove scraps from inside before setting off!

Old stone town is a fascinating place to get completely lost in the narrow streets, bustling with activity and spicy smells. The famous Zanzibar 'door' can be seen at various ages (as well as the reproduction). Apparently, the giant spikes on the heavy doors were to discourage elephants from trying to turn in the narrow streets and destroy their front doors!!!

Social life can be restricted in this Muslim dominated town, and we were visiting during Ramadan which is the Muslim festival of fasting where they can not eat, drink or smoke during daylight hours. It seemed incredible in this heat that they are not even allowed to drink water during the day and so they are not very friendly to tourists who are seen to be taking pleasure in any of these activities. It is best at this time to head for the North of Zanzibar for some serious 'chilled out' beach life. Ras Nungwi is a great anchorage in the Southeast season, with white sand beaches, turquoise waters and 'backpacker' style bars. From here we decided to head to the islands of Pemba nearby.

Pemba is an isolated Island with many small 'islets' surrounding it. Good snorkelling, breath-taking scenery and little else makes it definitely worth a visit. We certainly did have some exciting times navigating the area with the limited charts available. We quickly found out that the charts are not that accurate when they mark the depths and position of the reef, and I clearly remember getting the yacht quite 'stuck' when we literally ran out of water! I was hanging over the side of the bowsprit looking down into the clear water, watching the depth getting shallower and the reef closer to the bottom of the boat! We could not steer the boat in reverse exactly the way we had entered the reef, so the only way out was to jump in the water with a snorkel and navigate our way around the reef that way! At one point we had 4 divers in the water shouting instructions to me that I was relaying to Graeme on the helm. We were always extra cautious when we entered these islands and that was perhaps another reason we never saw any other yachts in the area.

Diary excerpt 23rd October 1999

Zanzibar lived up to expectations, Stone Town was fascinating and the famous 'street market' food was incredible, and we were anchored right next to it! After a week of exploring and topping up our trading items of batik and some bead jewellery, we left again for the sanctuary of a beach on the North tip of the island. Raz Nungwi was a beautiful beach, with white white sand and a collection of nice bars and people. We met 3 American guys, Jim, Jay and Lioness who joined us as paying crew to explore Pemba and passage back to Mombassa. Good company and good crew.

Mkoni,Pemba seemed like a never ending round of immigration and charges, with little of interest. We spent most of the time in very basic hot huts looking across at the customs officers and painfully slowly getting our passports checked and stamped. The officers would write so slowly and then go into a kind of trance while they tried to remember what they were suppose to be doing next! We headed for a small nature reserve island called Msaki, which looked beautiful but they wanted to charge us $30 to anchor and $5 per person to stay there, looking back now you'd think it would be worth that much, but we were on such a tight budget we would never consider spending that kind of money just to anchor. So we moved onto Wete, a small fishing town with a good market and we managed to get some beef, although we questioned whether it was Zebu which is the cow-like animal with a large hump. People were very friendly, although immigration was the usual pain! We then headed for the Northern tip and the most incredible white sand beach. Mostly uninhabited except for a small fishing village and the odd white Peace Core doctor and teachers. We chilled out very nicely for a couple of days, cooking fresh lobster bought from the fishermen on the beach.

Excerpt of letter to Bea 1st November 1999

"We picked up 3 American chaps North of Zanzibar and they cruised with us for 7 days around Pemba and back to Mombassa. We found a stunning white sand beach on the Northern tip of Pemba (2 miles long and deserted) and the local fishermen visited our yacht every morning with their catch, we ate like kings! Octopus and lobster cooked on the beach with coconut rice (made with fresh coconut of course) and salad. What a treat, we bought 7 lobsters between the 5 of us for under $5!"

So we continued to cruise from Mombassa, North to Kilifi and Lamu and South to Zanzibar and Pemba, picking up paying crew when we could to top up the cruising kitty and carry out the necessary repairs ready for our trip across the Indian Ocean.

Excerpt of letter to Bea 29th November 1999

We're now settled in 'Kilifi Creek' 25 miles north of 'Mtwapa Creek' but expect to keep commuting between the two. Mtwapa is much prettier, more lush with a lot more colour from the flowers, but Kilifi is the home of quite a few other 'yachties' and it makes a nice change to have 'like' people around you. We also have the facilities of a workshop with electricity to do some more work on the boat and also a place where we can dry out the boat to check the bottom. It looks like it's not going to be too difficult to earn money with paying crew either. We just did a trip for 7 days for 4 people to Lamu, which is a group of islands 100 miles north, including Manda Toto Island. It was a very good sail up there and only took 17 hours, but 2 of the girls got sea sick and one of them got off the boat at Lamu and didn't want to get back on! Still, the 2 Danish were very happy and would have stayed with us longer if they had more time.

The journey back was against the current with heavy rain and lightning (with no wind), so it took twice as long, arriving back at Kilifi at 4 a.m. It seems that the 'short rains' have arrived at last, which I think is a good thing for Kenya as there are many stories in the newspapers of areas struck by famine because of the droughts. When it rains, it really does rain, then it passes and you're left with no wind, and a very still hot atmosphere.

Other cruisers we meet are raising a family and working for the United Nations

We've met some really nice people on the yacht next to us, from Ripon in England, called Nick and Sue. They have been here for 3 years because Sue had an unexpected baby and little Jo is now 17 months old and quite a character, running around the boat and playing in the sea all the time, he seems very happy.

Gary and Jen are Australian and have been here for a couple of years. Gary has been working for the UN on food distribution for famine areas and earns quite a lot of money doing so. The UN

40

pays him 'danger money' since he has to go unaided into the jungle for periods of time and lead an expedition team of locals to find the food dropped by helicopters and then carry it to the various famine areas that need relief. Jen was always frantic with worry when he left on an expedition and I told Graeme in no uncertain terms that no money was worth that kind of worry. They were saving for a bigger boat as theirs is only a tiny 26 feet which they sailed from Australia in (rather them than me). It makes us feel very lucky to have found such a big boat; we still admire her all the time and thank our lucky stars.

Graeme is in the process of designing a self-steering wind-vane for the boat so that we don't have to hand-steer on the wheel 24 hours a day, which should make passages more comfortable. I'm in the process of being truly self-sufficient for our trip to Chagos (British Indian Ocean Islands), as there is nothing there at all. Jen is showing me how to bottle and can meat and vegetables and I'm busy brewing rice wine. We've got 3 months here before we set off again in February or March, so I'm making the most of the spare time.

Don't get Malaria in the UK

We found out after we left Kilifi that bad luck had befell Nick and Sue and little Jo. First Sue visited England and came down with Malaria whilst she was there. In East Africa this would not have been a problem since there is a well known cure for all strains of Malaria which is currently being tested in this area (at the time of writing it had not been approved by the FDA so could only be bought in East Africa where it was going through the human trial period). This wonder drug, called Cotextin, was readily available, as was a simple blood test to check if you had Malaria, in Kilifi (or the whole of East Africa), but was not available in England.

Unfortunately for Sue, Malaria is a tropical disease which is unfamiliar to the hospitals there, and so she kept being referred to special centres for tropical diseases until it was almost too late. This was very frustrating for her since she recognised immediately she had the symptoms for Malaria and kept insisting to the doctors this was her diagnosis, which they would not agree with. In England it can take 2 weeks to get the results of a blood test, by which time her organs had started to fail. She did eventually make a recovery after a lengthy hospital stay, but swore to take cotextin tablets with her if she ever made a trip away from East Africa again. The other yachties took her advice and we all added cotextin to our medical boxes on the boat.

But getting Malaria in East Africa is the safest place to get it

This is something I was very grateful for because I came down with Malaria a little while later in Tanga. I'd spent a really uncomfortable night and I felt really uneasy when I woke in the morning. I told Graeme I didn't feel good and had a really pounding head and we decided it would be wise to visit town and get a blood test for malaria. I took a Cotextin tablet anyway since it is harmless to take since it is actually a herbal remedy from the bark of a tree and a Chinese cure 2000 years old. It starts to work immediately on killing the parasite and the longer you leave it the least effective it can be. The blood test was very easy, cheap and safe and I waited in the little lab behind a shower curtain, whilst the technician tested my blood immediately for the parasite.

When I walked into the waiting room and told Graeme it was positive, he then went for a test, together with 2 other yachtie friends which were with us. The problem with malaria is that if someone near you has it, it has a good chance of being passed on since the mosquito can bite the infected person and transmit it immediately to the next person, with the next bite! The following day we told everyone we had come in contact with at the Tanga yacht club to go and have a test, and found that this was the site of infected mosquitoes. Worth bearing in mind next time you hear of someone close to you that has been infected.

Some time after Sue recovered from Malaria and returned to Kilifi, a terrible accident befell Nick when he was helping someone in a house with a light fixing. The electricity in East Africa is not to be trusted, with bad wiring and no safety standards, and Nick received an electric shock which instantly killed him. We heard that Sue and little Jo returned to England, their dreams shattered.

A reminder to live life to the maximum because you never know what is going to happen.

Diary excerpt 30th December 1999.

So Christmas has come and gone already! After Mtwapa we stayed in Kilifi for a couple of weeks and it was nice to see other yachties again, but we soon got tired of the long hikes into the nearest market to get provisions. We were beginning to think about the Millennium and if we could take advantage of the occasion to get some special paying crew to do a trip, when Bruno (a local crew member on a German boat), suggested Tiwi beach, which was popular with backpackers. We spent the day talking to the backpackers, most of which had already made special millennium plans, but we did meet Brownyn and Emmet who were really keen, if only we could find more people to share the cost. We met in Mombassa the following day and found 'the boys', Jerker, Rasmus, Tobius (brothers), and their friend Robert (from Finland and Sweden). They were a great comedy act and made a really great 10 day trip to Pemba and Zanzibar. It was good sailing and everyone got on and joined in really well. We had a fabulous dolphin show the first morning we arrived at Pemba, with 50 or 60 playing in the bow wave for a good half hour. The guys wanted to swim with the dolphins, which we didn't think was possible, but they did all jump in, and indeed, did swim with the dolphins! A day stop at Njao gap and then onto the 'hotel California' of Funzi Island (Pemba), a real paradise with great snorkelling, a white beach, and clear water, with an incredible sunset silhouetted by tall palm trees, everyone really enjoyed themselves!

A quick stop at Mkoni for customs and immigration, who this time tried to wangle $55 out of us! Considering last time we paid less than a dollar per person, we were not happy and complained until they accepted $14 for all of us with much negotiation! The fishing village was as delightful as I remembered it last time. Then to Zanzibar, where everyone agreed Raz Nungwi would be the place to celebrate the Millennium.

Millennium 2000 celebrations

We took a night sail first to stone town 'to do' immigration and get diesel, and for the benefit of the guys who were on a tighter time scale and had not visited stone town. Everyone was in really high spirits and looking forward to returning to Raz Nungwi for New Years Eve. The celebrations pretty much started before the International Date Line and by 6 p.m. we were in full flow, dressing the guys in my clothes and forming quite an array of breasts from

43

coconut shells. Even Emmet wore a dress, although he and Chris changed back into 'normal' clothes before going ashore. What a party we looked! Rasmus dressed in my Polka dot lycra dress looked nothing short of an attractive woman with his long thick blond hair, Toby sported the most magnificent Marilyn Monroe breasts in my halter neck top and Jerker looked plain 'gay' with his bald head. Graeme was definitely the 'belle' of the ball wearing my white velvet bodice top with firm coconut breasts and his green underpants – he got free drinks all night! We had quite the party and a memorable experience.

Bruno, from Africa (who came along as crew for the trip, after his job had finished on the German boat) managed to spoil things a little by stomping his feet and demanding to stay with his 'brother and sister' Julie and Graeme for the rest of his life, otherwise the 'mafia' may have to intervene. The East African still maintain a very paternalistic relationship with the whites and much prefer the lifestyle they led when the English aristocrats gave them their own quarters in their homes for their families in exchange for light cleaning, cooking and gardening. Their life under the British rule and the 'queen' gave them all more money, food and better health care, and they seem to aspire to this way of life again, always trying to find work with a family to provide for them. We often came across locals who asked us when our Queen would return to rule them! Unfortunately, the present President does very little to help the under privileged, keeping the riches for himself and his own family.

It spoilt the relationship a bit, but he had been spoilt by everyone on the boat and not asked to do any work, and he didn't want his life to change. When we returned to Mtwapa we helped him find another job as crew on a different boat, learning a lesson about providing employment for the locals.

Diary excerpt:

This will be our last trip in Africa, so plans are underway to cross the Indian Ocean, the grand plan being to head for the Seychelles, Chagos and then Thailand. I'm really looking forward to visiting those places but still feel quite apprehensive about the sailing. Will I ever get used to it?

Chapter 4 - The Indian Ocean - 6 months at sea.

"There is nothing so desperately monotonous as the sea, and I no longer wonder at the cruelty of pirates" James Russell Lowell

East Africa

By the time we had arrived in East Africa, we had made up our minds to head across the Indian Ocean to Thailand. I had already learnt a lot from other 'yachties', particularly in South Africa, but now the hard work really did begin. Khulula did not have refrigeration and so all the food we took must last for 6 months without refrigeration and needed some careful planning. We needed to take into account water and propane gas supplies for 6 months and storage for the maximum amount of diesel possible to see us through the 'doldrums'. The reason we were going to take 6 months was that we intended to stay in 'Chagos', which were uninhabited islands, for the maximum time of 3 months.

Excerpt from letter to Bea:

"We will take 1,600 litres of water from Mtwapa (Kenya), 31 litres of propane gas, 800 litres of diesel, 100 kilos of flour, 75 kilos of sugar, 50 kilos of rice, 50 packets of 250g Pasta, 5 kilos of coffee, 2,000 tea bags, 20 kilos of onions, half a ton of potatoes, 10 kilos of garlic, 10 kilos of mostly green tomatoes, 12 kilos of margarine, 20 litres of cooking oil and over 500 tins of canned vegetables and other foods. I'm also taking 300 fresh eggs which I have to individually coat in Vaseline to prevent air entering the shell and thus preventing bacteria too (I have arranged to collect these from a farm that guarantees freshness)

It takes quite a long time to calculate what you need (i.e. if you want fresh bread every other day that's how you calculate how much flour, yeast etc you need), and then to find the best place to buy it (we try and find bulk wholesalers), and how to get it back to the boat, and where to store it all (and you asked in your last letter what do we do for entertainment!). I've just filled 20, 20 litres barrels with all the rice and flour etc and left a white trail of hand and foot prints all over the boat! Tomorrow I start more serious 'bottling' – we've now successfully bottled 9 jars of fillet steak (see why do we need refrigeration?) and I want to try some more jam (mango this time), and pickle some eggs and maybe onions... so much to do! What would we do without our pressure cooker? (I guess we would need a fridge...)

I met quite a few other 'yachties' at Tanga who all swapped recipes for preserving food – it's very entertaining spending an evening swapping ideas and recipes whilst the men discuss boat maintenance and winds and currents! Certainly more entertaining than discussing what was on television or what you did in the office! We've become quite friendly with a couple who are going to the same places as us – some they have already visited and some the same as we've already visited – we spend many evenings swapping stories of where we've been and what we've seen, and tips on where we're going – plus swapping charts, looking at their photos etc. We're NEVER bored and certainly don't miss Television or Radio, not when we have a complete arena surrounding us of a constantly changing back garden!

We also read a lot (when we have time), and now have a completely new library of 30 or 40 books swapped with other yachties. We've actually met about 20 or so other yachties also going to Chagos (some already left, some already there), so we'll have lots of friends when we get there, as well as making new ones, no doubt! We're looking forward to learning all about fishing (fresh fish everyday in Chagos). We're not very good at catching, but they'll be plenty of other yachties to teach us all about spear-fishing and trawling and line-fishing, as well as, crab hunting and coconut harvesting. Because Chagos is ONLY accessible by yacht, it is quite a community and we expect up to 50 yachts there by the time we arrive (although there are so many islands you could lose yourself when you want to be alone.)

I never imagined that the first leg of this passage would take 35 days.

Coetivy, Seychelles, Indian Ocean – 1st stop after 5 days leaving Kenya

We could not make our first land fall of Pralin in the Seychelles, since the wind was pushing us south and further from this destination, so we headed for the most southern atoll of the Seychelles called Coetivy. We suspected we would not be allowed ashore because the official check-in with immigration has to be done 600 miles north on Mahe, the Capital island, but a Captain we met in Africa had told us they were very friendly to him when he visited and allowed him ashore.

Excerpt from letter to Bea:

"Graeme celebrated his 40th birthday anchored off one of the most southern Seychelles islands called Coetivy, it is a private island owned by a prawn farm with 200 inhabitants employed by the factory. Unfortunately we were not allowed ashore but we had a nice rest for 5 days whilst waiting for the wind. A couple of boats came out to visit us and one man promised to post our letters – but never returned. The 'Island Manager' did not want us on his island and I think perhaps he saw the visitors and told them not to return to us. All I wanted to do was walk on land, but I had to wait another 30 days until we got to Chagos before I would get that privilege!

Reading this letter jogged my memory but I couldn't remember WHY they wouldn't let us ashore, so I emailed Graeme and this was his reply:
"The trip to Chagos is easy... nothing happened, we drifted in the right direction for 30 days..., we baked a different dish every day, I got a bottle of Guinness on my birthday at Coetv but they wouldn't let us land unless we had weed to sell, and loose women on board. We caught an ugly fish. Memory jogged?"
He was right. It did jog my memory and I definitely remember feeling very indignant when the first boat arrived and asked if we were 'a couple'. It seemed like an odd question at the time, but after we had several more visitors with the same odd questions, we eventually befriended a native long enough to pose the question. The riddle was finally laid to rest when a local, quite nonchalantly explained that the 'last boat' who visited these islands had a single female crew member who had been at sea a bit too long and was at that age of sexual experimentation. The Captain had made it quite clear there was to be no 'hanky panky' between them, so I guess she was quite sexually frustrated by the time they arrived at this island. The locals were happy to oblige and solve this young lady's problem, so they automatically assumed the next boat along may need similar help

In the same respect, our helpful previous Captain had a little 'stash' on board which he happily shared with the locals so that he wouldn't have to throw it overboard before making customs and immigration landfall in Africa. They too expected this Captain to show the same generosity (even though we did not possess any...) it was an easy mistake to make. This island, the most Southern Atoll of the Seychelles, is 600 miles south of the Capital Island and is not on a yacht's normal course across the Indian Ocean, so they were quite 'cut-off' as an Island. The last yacht that had visited with the frustrated crew and generous Captain was 18 months previous. They must have been full of anticipation and then disappointment when they saw our yacht drop anchor!

Incidentally, we did meet this yacht in Africa and we would like to pass on our gratitude for misleading us into visiting this 'very friendly island' by Jamie, the Australian, who may be reading (and laughing) should he ever get a copy of this book. He had lived very nicely off this island for 3 weeks, staying in different huts every night and making the most of the hospitality, promising to send another boat soon to visit them! His misguidance had altered our course to rest here, assuming we would receive a nice welcome too... It was a lesson well learnt and despite a funny story it is evidence how innocently a yacht can influence a whole remote island and affect the reaction the next yacht will receive. It also reminded me of the French owned island, Glorieuses, who would not entertain any private yacht landing on her island because of the attitude of the very famous 'Movie Star' who insisted on 'buying' the island because he was not allowed to land (see Chapter Three).

The Indian Ocean, 1st leg, Seychelles – Chagos, 30 days

We waited as long as we could for the winds to come back, but they never really did, so we spent the next 30 days drifting in the right direction with the current.

Excerpt from letter to Bea:

"I was pleased to see land after 5 weeks – we had very little wind and it was a very wearisome journey, days when we just 'bobbed' in the middle of the 'Indian Ocean', 1,000 miles from the nearest land, our only company dolphins and flying fish and nothing but Blue Blue sea, 12,000 feet deep. It would have been nice, many a time, to take a dip, but the sharks in that depth probably wouldn't turn down an opportune snack! Many other yachties do swim in

48

the deep blue – personally I didn't think it was worth the peril and so sea-water showers suffice when you need to cool down.
We saw some magnificent sunsets and sunrises – the best on a very tranquil day when the sea was like glass and the sun as it set, turned the water an incredible crimson. For a complete 360 degrees all shades of scarlet, ruby, amethyst, violet and pink reflected off the soft feathery clouds – it was truly stunning. That same night the sky was so clear the stars were extraordinarily bright, the Milky Way like a giant white bridge and the whole sky literally twinkling. We sat for two hours watching the fantastic light show – we're so lucky!

We often had dolphins visit us and one day we even saw a whale – the spray of water and it's back arching out of the water, it was quite a sight because of the absolute size of it – not the kind of thing you would want to get too close to the boat! I can only guess it was at least twice the size of our boat!

Being at sea for 30 days was an once-in-a-lifetime experience and I couldn't begin to catalogue some of the highlights. I was personally quite spellbound by flying fish and some of their antics, the way they hurtle across the waves, leaping from the apex of the white water, trailing water droplets, spreading their horizontal fins and taking flight above the waves for as far as 130 metres plus (indeed some did land in the boat which I tell in more detail later in this chapter). Seabirds often stopped by for a rest on the boat, and it brought to mind a particularly large bird who struggled to stay on the safety line by wrapping his webbed feet completely around the rope and then rocked forward and backward with the motion of the boat, desperately trying to stay put on semi-stable land as long as possible! We tried many antics to get him off the safety line, not only because he was making quite a mess, but because I was being distracted by him on night watch.

I also remember, quite vividly, the utter darkness of night watches particularly when cloud cover obliterated the horizon and stars making you feel very inconsequential in a colossal cosmos of blackness. I used to hate night watches and as the sun touched the horizon I was always left with a sense of the impending darkness which was about to descend like a prowler in the backyard. On nights like this you would plunge into total darkness, left with only a red glow from the compass light mesmerising you into a hypnotic state as you tried to stay on course. Time would slow right down making an hour or 2 hours seem like an eternity, forever checking the time and playing games with yourself to avoid the realisation only a few minutes had passed since the last time you checked. When the time eventually ticked by to change watch I would carefully note how long it would take Graeme to respond and try and figure in an extra five minutes to make a thermos flask for his watch (which meant my shift finished 5 minutes early to make his flask up). I never came to a fair use of the time between shifts to eat or drink; it always seemed such a waste of precious sleeping time.

Moreover I recall some of the strange UFO sightings, in the sea, as well as the sky. One particular episode I put down to giant squid signalling each other across the ocean with their bright effervescent lights at regular intervals. Phosphorescence is a phenomenon that is produced by plankton. This chemo luminescence is common to marine animals and is believed to be a protective reaction to danger and is likely to be the sanest explanation for the large bright spheres I saw.

One day, as dawn broke, I spotted a strange sight which looked a bit like the tops of palm trees floating on the horizon, which gradually formed into a group of sand spits topped with palm trees dotted across the horizon. After 5 weeks at sea, we had finally sighted Chagos, a really breathtaking landfall of 10 islands surrounding a lagoon approx 4 miles in diameter.

Salomon was our first landfall and it has become a yachtsmen's Mecca being one of the only places left on the planet which is totally uninhabited and quite inaccessible. The total Chagos Archipelago is actually scattered over an area of 54,389 square kilometres, with a total land area of only 60 square kilometres. Saloman and Peros Banhos atolls lay to the north, with Diego Garcia, the largest island, to the south across the Great Chagos Bank. It was first discovered by the Portuguese, and then settled by the French in 1776 that used it primarily as a leper colony. The Archipelago became British in 1814 and in 1970 the U.S leased Diego Garcia as a military base.

Today the only current population are the U.S. military and a handful of British administrators on Diego Garcia and there is no population on any of the other islands. Since Diego is quite a few hundred miles from the most northern islands where the yachts visited, we never saw anyone other than other yachties and coconut crabs. We did receive one visit in the 3 months we were there to have our passports stamped by the British Navy!

At its peak, the population was mostly Portuguese fishermen and lepers from Mauritius and were known as the Ilois. At the beginning of the 20th century there were 450 families in residence, which was soon depleted by the spread of leprosy. The islands were then known as 'The oil islands' named for the oil extracted from the copra, which is the dried meat of the coconut.

When the US took control of Diego Garcia as a military base, the population of all the islands were removed back to Mauritius causing quite a stir amongst the islanders, some of which were 5th generation. Eventually, after many court battles and human rights protests, the islanders were compensated by the British government, but are still not allowed to return to the islands to visit the graves of their loved ones. As a result of no population being present for nearly 40 years, each anchorage off the islets was pure white sand beaches and overgrown lush palm trees, a real picture postcard of unspoilt splendour. No fishing is allowed in the waters and so the coral is pristine and the fish abundant.

Church ruins, Bodum, Chagos

Laundry Day, Bodum, Chagos

Mercedes and Ronan, Tommy and Sandra
and Author, Ille de Pass, Chagos
Ronan shows his injury from a trigger fish.

Hunting coconut Crabs, Ille de Pass, Chagos

Diary notes from Chagos

BODUM - situated in the Salomon atoll. The island of ruins.

This island still has some ruins of the last inhabitants, which make captivating exploring. I think what makes it more fascinating is the way the jungle has completely taken over the ruins and added an almost supernatural magnificence to the place. Although it is nearly 40 years since the last people lived here, the old wells still provide brackish fresh water - ideal for showering or doing the laundry!!! All that remains is the front wall of the church, an overrun graveyard, and even more overgrown school house.

The inside of the Island has very few ruins, the large palm trees entirely dominating the interior, and the only inhabitants being outsized coconut crabs which have front claws the size of my forearm, and stronger than the human jaw. They are evident by the large piles of coconut husks outside their hideouts - and if you are interested to see them up close they can be coaxed out of their dens by a stick employed into the entrance.

The view from the beach belongs on a postcard, crystal clear water, well-preserved coral gardens, and a startling diversity of multi-coloured fish and palm trees swaying in the breeze. This place really is seventh heaven, and we were delighted to be able to sail everywhere in our mirror dinghy and investigate around the shoreline.

ILLE DE PASS – Island of the colossal Coconut crabs

This small island situated in the 'pass' of the Salomon atoll, was rarely visited, but had the largest population of coconut crabs, of all sizes, that we had seen. The jungle here is denser, but a glade had already been cleared, which we adopted as our base camp for a few weeks. Our group consisted of Mercedes and Ronan (English and French), Kevin and Sue (South African), Tommy and Sandra (German) and ourselves. We made a good amalgamation of diverse desert island skills, and pooled our resources to eat the major meal at our encampment everyday. Tommy was an exceptional fisherman, and always had a good catch of coral trout, red snapper or grouper. Sandra was an extraordinary bread maker, which she cooked in a cast-iron pot on the camp-fire by

54

stacking the hot ashes on the lid and around the pot. Everyday she came up with a new recipe - fresh coconut, onion bread, garlic bread, etc. Mercedes made the most inconceivable ginger beer (despite her recipe I still can't reach her quality), and Ronan was dependable for the larger fish catch by trolling with his dinghy (yellow-fin tuna). Sue had a hoard of remarkable pickled vegetables, and was still the best at sprouting mung-beans for the salad, whilst Kevin made some really mean brews with orange peel and anything he could get his hands on!!!!

We became the 'pub' with interesting fruit wines made from a bag of out-of-date dried fruit, and rice-wine which I had become quite the expert at brewing. Graeme became the authority on harvesting the heart of the Palm - the only 'fresh' vegetable, apart from sprouts, available to us. We all really enjoyed this time together, and it holds fond memories for us all.

TAKAMAKA & FOUQUET – A visit by the 'round the world millennium yacht race'

The two most strikingly beautiful islands in the Salomon group was the beach chosen for the 'Millennium round the world yacht race" beach barbecue. I think all the yachts at Salomon where surprised to see 4 identical 65ft racing boats anchoring for a few days R&R, obviously stocked up with cold beer, meat and probably fresh vegetables!!!!! I think everyone made it clear to them that our diet of fish, rice, coconut and home-made wine could be supplemented with a few of the luxuries on their boats, in exchange for our island knowledge! We showed them how to recognize drinking coconuts (and how to get them, and open them), eating coconuts, heart of palm and how to find the coconut crabs!

We also supplemented their barbecue with fresh fish of all varieties, lobster, octopus and squid. We were invited aboard 'Spirit of Diana' for Roast Lamb dinner the following day, much to our delight, and left with multi-vitamin tablets and a bottle of red wine (and what was left of a large bottle of scotch whiskey).

PEROS ATTOL – The impenetrable islands

Much quieter than Bodum, this atoll is larger, but with a restricted number of wells and very little sign of any habitation. Most of the islands are impenetrable because the palm trees are so dense, but still offer the same beautiful clear waters and marine life. One morning we woke to find a large manta ray (2m wing span) swimming around the yacht. We watched it for over 20mins elegantly gliding and somersaulting for our entertainment. From the sea, whichever island, on whichever atoll, they all look pretty much the same - very flat, other than the dense palm-trees, bright white beaches and crystal clear turquoise waters. I can't wait to go back!!!!!!!

Excerpt from letter to Bea:

The islands are so beautiful and abundant with birds and fish and coconut palms and coconut crabs – pre-historic giant crabs that feed exclusively on coconuts which they break open with their huge claws – I have never seen anything like it! We went 'hunting' with our friends that we met up with again here, Ronnie and Jenny (who we originally met in Tanga) Jenny is quite incredible, she is Thai and like a little monkey climbing trees to harvest the coconut and completely fearless. She just stands on the back of the crab, grabs its huge claws and ties them with palm leaves to immobilise them, then marches them straight to the beach fire, absolutely delicious!

They also showed us how to harvest 'heart of palm' which is a wonderful crisp white 'vegetable ', a cross between radish and white cabbage, which you can make a very tasty salad from. It is the base of the palm tree and you have to keep trimming the 'husk' to get to the 'heart'. You get quite a large 'heart' from a small palm tree and it is the only 'fresh' vegetable which you can get on the islands. We still have onions, garlic and potatoes which we bought in Kenya, but 6 weeks later the tomatoes need using quickly now for cooking and the potatoes are going quickly too. Still, there's always plenty of fish and crab which you catch fresh everyday. It really is quite a life living on a desert island and we feel very privileged to be here......

....by the time we had left we had learnt so many 'island skills' for survival (we would have no problem with those survivor series that they have on the television). Graeme was often found marching into the jungle, with machete in hand, to hunt a coconut crab and chop down a young palm tree to get to the 'heart of palm'. We

also feasted on quite a variety of fish from line-fishing off the boat, as well as lobster (usually speared by someone else).

We were invited along one day to watch some other yachties spear-fishing and I found the whole experience quite frightening! The sound of the spear in the water attracts sharks and they will happily circle around whilst you hunt for the fish or lobsters. I had already been warned of the sharks and told not to panic under any circumstances but to either ignore the sharks or growl or be aggressive towards them. Well, when one of the spears found a large grouper fish one of the sharks decided they wanted it for dinner and chased the swimmer to the surface! I'm afraid I panicked and starting splashing in the water to get back to the dinghy! Jenny came to my rescue and I nearly drowned her struggling to get out of the water! Everyone found my reaction quite amusing, but at least I distracted the shark away from the swimmer! Needless to say I didn't go along to watch the spear-fishing again. There was an incident a few years earlier when a spear-fishing yachtie lost an arm to a shark in a similar incident, I heard the tale told around the fires and just assumed it was one of those fishing stories, but now I wasn't so sure!

I even collected 'clams' on the beach, small, but very tasty! But we soon ran out of the fresh vegetables we bought from Mombassa and our only other vegetable was 'bean-sprouts' which were ready every 2-3 days with continuous 'sprouting' from the mung-beans we bought from Africa. They made an excellent salad with the 'heart of palm' together with onions and garlic which we still have. As the weeks went by more and more trading took place between the yachts, some trading cigarettes for garlic, beer for rice or flour for salt, it made for an interesting barter market over the vhf radio every morning. Coconuts were a-plenty and we learnt which were best for drinking (young and green and usually still on the tree), and eating (older and usually fallen), even a delicious meat can be found from the sprouting coconut.

I continuously brewed and Khulula became quite popular for our varieties of home-made wine. I managed to produce 80 litres from one kilo of dried fruit, which was definitely the best! My other speciality was rice wine, made from rice and sugar and yeast (and a handful of raisins). Each yacht had their speciality and we met an English girl, married to a French man, who made the most excellent ginger-beer. Mercedes and Ronan became good friends

*and we we're sorry to go our separate ways (they arrived from
Thailand on-route to Africa, so we had lots of stories to swap).
The last few weeks we were in a group of 4 yachts and the 8 of us
met every day for 'communal' meals. It worked very well as
everyone produced one dish, so there were 4 dishes each meal to
share.*

*By the time we left, the sea was a lot cooler and with days of rain,
there were less opportunities to snorkel and swim (a shame
because the coral was quite spectacular)."*

Addu, Maldives, Indian Ocean

Eventually the change in weather and lack of provisions told us it
was time to move onto to our next leg of the journey across the
Indian Ocean to Thailand, but first, we took a small detour to
Addu, for a little limited provisioning and re-fuel with diesel.

Excerpt from letter to Bea:

*"It's incredible that Addu (the most Southern Atoll of the Maldives)
is only 300 miles further North of Chagos, but considerably hotter.
We're really pleased to be exposed once more to shops and the
little luxuries like fresh eggs, vegetables and chicken, which are
really special. The people are very friendly, mostly Sri-Lankan
and East Indians, working in the 4 textile factories here (one of
which is Victoria's Secret). We've made friends with the
'Cafeteria' management who cater for 1300 employees providing
all the meals for the workers, tonight we are invited for 'dinner'.
They have also offered us the use of their bicycles so that we can
visit some of the other islands in the atoll, they look quite beautiful,
but 13 kms to the furthest island is a bit too far to walk (that would
be 26kms in one day), so we'll try the bikes and see how far we
can get......."*

We were very impressed by the islands we visited, each
connected by a causeway to the main island with the factories.
The streets were spotlessly clean with the little yards of each
small house swept fresh and tidy. The children waved and smiled
and the adults shyly acknowledged us with a polite greeting. We
only got as far as 2 islands because we were so distracted by
another little store we found that sold frozen buffalo and had just
received a new shipment of fresh vegetables. We didn't have

enough cash to buy all the fresh produce we would have liked so we proposed a 'trade' for some of the canned produce we had on our boat. They were very pleased to make the exchange and we agreed on bringing some canned vegetables which we could exchange for apples and oranges and potatoes. Each day we walked to the island with another backpack of cans and exchanged them for fresh produce.

The rules and regulations were quite strict on the island, being austerely Muslim, and the locals did not like to be seen socialising or spending too much time with the white boat people. In fact, the one evening we convinced the Cafeteria Management to visit our boat for a return meal; we had to sneak ashore in the dark to collect them from the beach, because it was declared 'illegal' to visit a foreign yacht.

Excerpt from letter to Bea:

…We are both very well, although we were conscious of the fact our diet in the last 3 months lacked a lot of vitamins and minerals you get from fresh vegetables and meat, also rain-water lacks the minerals you usually get so that doesn't help (but it tastes so sweet..). We were fortunate that the 'Round the World Millennium Yacht race' called in at Chagos, all British, and very kind to us, donating vitamin supplements and a very nice bottle of red wine (we're not sure which we were more delighted with!) Obviously the wine is long gone but we're still taking the 'one-a-day'.

We're stocking up well for the journey to Thailand (we expect it to take a couple of weeks) so I'm busy again bottling meat and we should be able to get cabbage and potatoes to see us through, maybe some fruit for the first few days, but it doesn't keep. So we'll probably be in Thailand by August. We're both really looking forward to a different culture and some three dimensional scenery!

The Indian Ocean – 2nd leg, Maldives to Thailand, 1584 miles, 17 days.

This time I thought I would keep myself occupied at sea by writing a daily diary which I could then send to all my friends and relatives when we arrived, to give them an idea of what it is like being at sea for long periods of time.

12th July 2000, 4.00 p.m. 1583.94 miles to Phuket, Thailand

A perfect sea and a perfect sail! After some delay leaving Addu Atoll (Gan), in the Maldives, we're on the way! If sailing was like this all the time you wouldn't want to worry about how long it will take to get anywhere. It's truly beautiful, a cooling breeze, a gentle swell and just the sounds of the sea.

We were delayed by our anchor getting fouled on an old anchor chain on the sea-bed and following 6 hours yesterday trying to retrieve it ourselves, we eventually had to pay for a diver - $40!! That leaves our funds to arrive in Thailand at the grand sum of $150! Hopefully money will meet us there from England, but we're told it's cheap in Thailand anyway, so I'm sure it won't be a problem!

13th July 2000, 0929 a.m. Khulula crosses the equator!

We're bombing along at 8 knots with a 30 knot wind (and no rain). We didn't see a sign, or dotted line or join mark and we've crossed from winter to summer (so where's the sun?) You'd expect something to mark crossing the centre of the earth wouldn't you? So we're now up-side-down and climbing up hill!

5.30p.m. same day, 1487 miles to go

Lying-a-hull in the rain (Again). The same happened last night about the same time – no wind – so you put the sails away, then gusting wind (so you say, 'sod it, I didn't want to get wet anyway') Anyway, it's dinner time, Tuna curry tonight, last night Buffalo stew, compliments of my busy 'bottling' whilst in Addu, quite marvellous, bottled meals (who needs tins or refrigeration?) I've bottled Buffalo, chicken and fish, soup and curry, just add a few vegetables (potatoes and cabbage because they last best), garlic, ginger, onions, herbs and spices – Presto! We're actually eating better at sea than we did on land! I got the idea from another yacht (posh one)who made meals, froze them, and then whammed them in the microwave at sea – but hey – that's the normal way, and Khulula has it's own bottling and brewing factory, so who needs gadgets? (Other than the pressure cooker of course!)

14th July – 1390 miles to go – 10.30 p.m.
Writing in the moonlight on watch. The sky has cleared and the
wind has gone completely so we've been motoring most of the
day, and probably night. We saw a really beautiful 360 degree
sunset from flaming reds to purples and pinks and as it's just
before full moon which looked like a bright white ball against a
cerise sky. The sea is so tranquil it's the colour of gunmetal and
reflects the moon and the colours of the sky like a mirror – not a
ripple to spoil the picture. I had a baking day today, so we had fruit
scones with home-made mango, apple and strawberry jam with
our last tin of cream – yum, yum! We've got 'English Muffins' for
breakfast (or watch snacks) which takes less time to bake than
bread (and we only have half a bottle of propane to last us, so
gas-easy meals are important).

We both managed to do some reading today and both enjoyed
fresh water showers (compliments of all that bloody rain). So all
we need now is some wind! Thank god for the diesel we bought
in Gan, it was a wise decision to blow the last of our money to fill
up the tanks (500 litres), so we could motor through the doldrums
until we pick up the trade winds. Bobbing and drifting can drive
you nearly insane when you haven't got the luxury of motoring
(like the Mombassa-Chagos passage). Sailing though is much
more comfortable (you don't get slammed so much by waves), so
the sooner the better.

In case you didn't realise we don't have auto-pilot, so we hand-
steer 24 hours along with various techniques to enable you to
write at the same time (i.e. steer with your feet, tie the wheel if the
boat is balanced). We take it in turns to be on watch, usually
Graeme does 3 hours and then I take over for 2 hours to allow him
to sleep (and that for 24 hours continuous) For this passage
though we made some new rules, it there is no wind and we're
tired, we go to sleep and let the boat drift, if it's squally and horrid
outside, close the hatch and let the boat drift, if we both get really
tired and there is wind we 'hove to' (you set the sails for a
controlled drift) After all, what's the rush?

July 16th 3.40 a.m. – 1291 miles to go.

So we've been drifting since I came off my last watch at 12.30
a.m. We had a good day sailing all day and the wind died on

61

Graeme's first watch, so we motored until 12.30 then decided there was no use driving when we could be sleeping! Graeme still stayed up on watch though (keeping a look-out for ships etc.) A really huge container ship passed close-by yesterday morning so we're in 'shipping lanes' at the moment.

We were rewarded with a royal dolphin show last night, just before sunset, they are attracted to the 'bow-wave' of the boat and play a 'dare' game diving across the front of the boat as it crashes into the waves, these were particularly playful, small with long noses and a tri-colour body (lightest on the belly) and are called 'spinners' because of the way they leap really high out of the water vertically and then spin several times in the air. They played with us for a good 20-30 minutes and then all dashed off, leaping out the water.

Shortly afterwards we had a catch on the fishing line (tuna of course) but unfortunately lost it as Graeme was trying to land it – it's not easy when your sailing along trying to land from 2 metres from the water-line. A real shame since we seem to have mastered the art of tuna biltong – great tasty snacks – you soak small strips of raw tuna for 12 hours in soy sauce and coriander and then hang up in the sun and wind for 2 days to dry, then munch – yum yum! Oh well, maybe another time! Well, it looks like the wind is on the way back so I'll give Graeme another half hour to make sure it's blowing consistently then we'll set of again.

18th July 3.45 p.m. 1039 miles to go.

Hooray for the trade winds!! We're really making good progress now after a couple of frustrating days in Sri Lankan water after seeing nothing for days on end and enjoying the solitude, we suddenly had far too many frequent visits from Sri Lankan fishing boats. Big ugly loud wooden boats that make a bee-line for you to try and scrounge cigarettes, beer or anything else a rich white yachtie would have! They come really close holding up fish, and coconuts which they want to exchange for 'white' goods, and they won't go away until some trading has taken place. On one occasion we had 3 racing towards us to see who could get the closest and do a trade, nice enough chaps, but you can do without the open-market at sea! However, we did exchange some of our valuable possessions for a big yellow-fin tuna (which is now drying in the sun for biltong) and a packet of lemon-puff biscuits! We were only 120 miles off Sri-Lanka, so it did get quite busy! Now we seem to have passed the main fishing grounds, so hopefully, no more visitors!

This is great sailing, 7 knots in the right direction, only problem is it can get quite tiring and it's bloody hot. We've rigged a shade but it's still scalding hot!

19th July 7.15 p.m. – 927 miles to go.

We are definitely in the trade winds now, only problem being able to physically sail for 24 hours! It's pretty tiring on the helm in good winds like these, so last night we tried to get the most out of it by doing a 2:1 watch (I get the 2 hours sleep, one hour watch, Graeme the One hour sleep and the 2 hour watch). It worked until about the 3rd watch around 3a.m. when we were both suffering from sleep deprivation and short tempers! Tonight we've decided to have the 'night-off' or at least until our bodies tell us they have caught up on their sleep.

The moon is now in it's getting up later each evening cycle and it's not due tonight until 9.00 p.m. Its pitch black outside but I found once the eyes adjust the stars get quite bright. We're still in shipping lanes (south of the Bengal basin mouth), so we have to keep a watch all night, but at least we're not on the helm so you can write and read.

The sea in this area is quite strange, olive green, really a very dark green. I've never seen sea like it, up to 5,000 miles at sea have only been the bright blue variety, so I wonder what could be causing it to turn green? We did wonder if its air pollution from India, we have seen some very strange colours in the sky and the moon with 4 or 5 halos of green and pink! However, we have been told that the sea in Thailand is 'Emerald green' so what causes that? Still I'm sure Emerald green looks much nicer than 'olive green' It makes you think; we're so out of touch with the rest of the world that there could be a nuclear fall-out on land and we wouldn't know about it. Imagine arriving at land and yachties being the only survivors in the world. We'd survive pretty well with all the provisions we carry (usually enough for a year's supply of tins and staple food), but what a shock it would be to arrive at land and find it gone… (Mmm, the things you think about at sea…reminds me of a movie...

22nd July – 5.40 p.m. 683 miles to go.

We're still making good progress, but both very tired! We've taken to stopping whenever we both feel we need more sleep and this tends to mean around 20 hours underway a day. We've now put the clocks forward one hour(thought it was about time as it was getting light in the morning around 4.30 a.m. and we can decide ourselves at sea when to change the hour) We will need to put them ahead another hour before arriving in Thailand (7hr plus London)

The sea has returned to it's beautiful crystal blue (it's particularly beautiful at the moment) We're both really looking forward to getting back to land and things are beginning to run a bit short, looks like all the tank water has gone so we're on our emergency 100 litre deck water now, propane gas is likely to run out in the next day or so, half a tub of margarine (which is o.k. because we can't cook bread with no propane gas and anyway there is not enough flour left) sugar is down to half a tub, but there's still 15 litres of home-brew (ginger beer and pineapple wine) so the 'spirits' are still high!

26th July – 7.00a.m 304 miles to go.

We're both extremely tired and fatigued, days and nights have blurred into light and dark and we're so tired if we're not steering, we're sleeping! There is no time for anything else because as soon as it's your turn for a break from the helm, all you want to do is sleep! We're both looking forward to sleeping more than 2 hours at a time! No opportunities now to stop and rest as we're constantly have to keep watch for the busy 'Malacca straits' traffic, we've passed so many high container ships, the size of some are quite incredible, like small islands! One particularly large one we passed close by at night actually cut its engines to let us pass since we were travelling so slowly. Fortunately sailing vessels have right-of-way, so if they're in your path they have to change course (which most tend to do rather than stopping, although you do hear stories of container ships who keep a poor watch and run down a yacht without even knowing).

We also met another yacht at sea, the first time ever, so we motored over to say (shout) hello! They are also on the way to

Phuket although they are making better progress than us because their rig is more suited to this wind (wind mostly from behind and their sails were goose-winged to catch the wind) We've not spotted them since so we're calculating they are presently further east and North and will certainly arrive before us. They did throw us some old bread, which we were quite grateful for since we've now run out of propane gas and sugar and down to 80 litres of water. Graeme is trying to be very inventive with food; inventing combinations you can 'cook' in a flask of boiling water (instant potatoes are proving very popular). We have an electric kettle which we can boil when you switch the engine and generator on, so it's quite a task every time you want to boil the kettle!

We are expecting to see land today (Sumatra) and then it's into the busy Malacca straits which you cross to get to Phuket, Thailand. The straits are notorious for busy shipping and horrid weather, so we'll see what it has in store for us! So far we've been very lucky with the weather, this being the rainy season for Thailand, so we expected lots of rain (so far none, touch wood). I expect once we get closer to land we won't be so lucky! You can already see the clouds building, so it won't be long before we're sitting in the rain on the helm!

We have both said we will not do another long ocean passage without auto helm (or extra crew) whatever the cost! Hopefully 2 or 3 more days and we'll be in the land of 8 hour sleeps, cold beer and decent food!

28th July 1.40 a.m. – 142 miles to go (of torture!)

This is really horrid! We are in a patch of very turbulent sea which is bashing the boat around so much we can not steer under sail or motor, it's really frustrating. We've still been pretty lucky with the weather but the wind is 'up the bum' which is impossible for us to sail on, seems such a waste of good strong wind, but it only sends us in the wrong direction, so we keep having a 'break'. Graeme is asleep and I'm on watch until 2 a.m. We had anticipated arriving first light Saturday morning, but that won't happen if we don't start making some progress!

4.45 a.m. same day - still 139 miles to go
(3 miles since 1.40 am) How's that for progress? Now we've got the weather as well! High winds and squalls

29th July 8.50 p.m. – 11 miles to go!

So close and yet so far away! After a very exhausting night of hourly watches on the helm, to make the most of the squally wind, it was touch and go whether we would make the anchorage before night-fall. We made the decision at 3 p.m. to abandon all hope! Despite us only being 14 miles off we had no wind and were only achieving a pathetic 3 knots (making four and half hours to our destination). The entrance is not that easy, with reefs and shallows, so we don't want to navigate in the dark, so we're 'hove-to' drifting towards land and we'll plan to sail first light. It's extremely frustrating being able to see land and all the goodies that await us!

We virtually have no food left (at least that you don't need to cook) and yesterday the engine decided to stop working (hence the reason we can't motor to our destination) so we can't even boil a kettle! Graeme had a tin of cold vegetable curry for dinner, straight out the can, but I couldn't face it and decided to wait until we get to land tomorrow!

3rd August – anchored in Ao Chalong, Phuket, Thailand.

To finish the tale, it took even longer to get to land than we expected! That day we rested and set off again at 3 a.m., the wind died and then changed direction which meant making land was extremely difficult since it was blowing us away from land.

We eventually dropped anchor at 5 p.m. that day exhausted, frustrated and ready for that beer! It had taken us 20 hours to complete the last 11 miles without an engine so the warm welcome, a great meal and several cold beers were very welcome, before settling into our first full night's sleep for 17 days!!!

Never again.

Sailing the Indian Ocean and drying tuna

The Author in Phang Nga Bay, Phuket.

Chapter Five – A female nomad in Southern Thailand

"There are two choices. You can make a living or you can design a life" Jim Rohn

Phuket, our first land fall

Ao Chalong, Phuket, was our first land fall in Thailand and the thing that struck me more than anything was the three dimensional quality to the islands. They call Thailand 'land of the smiles' and this I would completely agree with. Following our long hard journey to get here, the welcome was warm and indisputable. I insisted we set off for shore almost immediately, beckoned by cold beer and fresh meat and vegetables (and cigarettes). This turned out to be no easy task, bearing in mind we had just done a major ocean passage, our dinghy was lashed to the deck and the rig lashed to the safety lines. We only had our hard sailing dinghy, which relied on wind to push us along, or short paddles when there was no wind (we didn't even have proper rowing oars). It would be an effort to get the dinghy in the water and then rig it up with the mast and sail ready to go ashore.

"It's worth the effort", I told Graeme, "There's a little wind and if we get be-calmed we could always paddle"

"Have you seen how far we are from the shore?" was Graeme's reply; it must have been close to a mile because this was a shallow bay which dried out.

"I'm not spending another evening without food, let's just do it"

So we did, and paddled some of the way. We headed for a bar/restaurant called Suda's Bar, which had been recommended to us by a couple we met in Chagos.

"They are really yachtie friendly there, with great cheap food and beer, fast internet access, use of the basic shower, laundry and a 'cruisers board' for information" Mercedes had told us.

Sure enough, Suda's welcome was incredible. We must have appeared quite dishevelled, and had no Thai baht to pay for anything, but despite this, we were given credit and a warm smile.

"Don't worry about the money, we're used to cruisers here who have just arrived from another country and spent many days at sea. Help yourself to anything on the menu and we'll start a tab for you. Welcome to Phuket" said Suda with a big smile.

This ended up being our 'home base' for over two years, and we returned Suda's goodwill many times over when we brought tourists, other cruisers, and guests to her establishment to buy food and drink and pay for the laundry or internet. This was the kind of business woman who knew how to run a successful business, but to her, she was just following the Buddhist way of life, to give unreservedly. Generally, we found this to be the case in the whole of Thailand, generous, warm, trusting people who didn't understand the concept of lying or deceit, bad manners or duplicity. Suda ended up giving us 2 weeks credit whilst we waited for money from the U.K. and we could have just sailed off anytime and disappeared, but it didn't even cross her mind that we would even consider doing a thing like that.

I once left my purse in the market and didn't miss it until several hours later when someone approached me in Suda's bar and asked if this was my purse. They had walked over a mile in the heat, and headed for the 'farangs' bar where they were likely to spot the stupid white farang that had left their purse behind! (Farang is Thai for white person).

And so, with Ao Chalong becoming our "home base" in Phuket, we started to explore the surrounding cruising ground.

Phang Nga Bay and the man with the golden gun

After seeing only flat Islands with palm-trees, the high limestone outcrops of the South Andaman Sea are fascinating, and Phang Nga Bay is an incredible inland sea of these outcrops, forming small islands and great sheltered anchorages.

Diary excerpt 14th June 2001

Koh Phanak in Phang Nga Bay is a steep island with a really deep high cave leading to an inland 'Hong' which is accessible at different tides. At high tide it is necessary to dive under the under-cut at the back wall of the cave, which is easy to spot because you can see the light shining up through the water. First time we came here I was nervous enough paddling the dinghy through the cave, it has a high roof and you are soon in complete darkness and all you can hear and smell are the bats. As you enter the cave from the sea, the cave takes a turn to the right, so this then blocks the light from the entrance. You just keep rowing in the dark, using flash-lights until the cave dead-ends and you spot the light from the 'Hong' shining up.

"How do you know how far you have to dive before you come up inside the Hong?" I asked Graeme, as he was contemplating diving under the undercut to investigate.
"I don't know, but I'll just feel my way and push myself against the roof until I reach fresh air", was Graeme's brave reply!

He lowered himself into the water, and I watched him disappear through the hole in the cave. An anxious wait inside the dark cave alone was interrupted a few minutes later.

"I got through to the Hong, it's a massive in-land lake with steep jungle cliffs surrounding it, and so we'll come back at a lower tide so you can explore it with me"

And that is exactly what we did do when we had some friends visit a few weeks later. We entered the cave at mid-tide, which gave us enough water in the cave to row the boat to the end of the cave, but low enough that the gap in the wall was exposed and you could see through the gap to the other side.
This meant I didn't have to dive under the undercut, just swim, taking care not to catch myself on the sharp oyster shells which lined the ceiling.

"Wow, this place is amazing, an inland lake which can only be entered from a cave" I exclaimed.
Apparently these hongs were discovered in World War 2 when the planes flew low to try and find prisoners of war which hid in the caves. They could see the hongs because the ceilings are exposed to the sky, so they could see 'down' inside the hongs. Apparently, 'Hong' is Thai for 'room', so a Hong is a room inside the mountain. This whole area was full of 'hongs', so we would have plenty of exploring to do, and we had a small hand-written guide which was given to us by some other cruisers we met in Chagos, to give us clues where to find the entrances.

One of the islands is named after the 'Hong', so it is called Koh Hong (Koh meaning island, so it is an island with a room). This Hong is reached by a large open cave which you can enter by dinghy from the sea at hide tide, and dinghy into the large inland lake (see photo opposite taken inside the cave).

Diary excerpt June 2001:

Koh Hong is one of the most striking hongs which we visited for the first time with Liz and Kendra. As we paddled through the large open cavern entrance, the emerald green inland lagoon came into view. It was surrounded by high sheer limestone cliffs with kingfishers diving from them. We tied the dinghy to an overhang and lowered ourselves into the emerald water and floated, looking up at the blue sky. We swam to the far side of the Hong and disturbed a giant water monitor who must have been six feet long (easy to mistake them for a crocodile, but they are not in these waters).

There is another Koh Hong in the area which is also a beautiful setting. This Hong is now quite open since the original high cave has been eroded by the sea, leaving two giant limestone outcrops in its place.

Diary excerpt June 2001:

Koh Hong, Krabi, is where we first spotted our 'cartoon' bird, which we decided was either an extinct species or maybe one not yet discovered. The colourful bird had a large head with an over-size beak, which looked a bit like a hornbill. It was very downy and vibrantly coloured scarlet and orange with a comparatively diminutive body and petite feet which seemed to defy gravity the way he was balanced on a twig. After much research we concluded it was some kind of kingfisher, but couldn't place this particular species.

Koh Khai had a fabulous 'over-hang' on the cliff face creating a canopy of stalagmites and stalactites which formed itself into an ingenious fairy tale palace complete with staircases, little castles with turrets and courtyards. Colossal crystal waterfalls cascade down the cliff front, frozen mid-flow, and shimmer as though the water still glistens.

72

The first time we visited, it was low tide, and we had to use ropes to climb up to the canopy to explore it. It was tough climb for a couple of our friends with us (and me) and we didn't want to abseil back down so we edged to the rim of the canopy and looked down to the ocean to see if jumping would be a better option. As we all stood on the rim looking down (maybe 30 feet down) a monster sea snake surfaced and surprised us with his size, it must have been over 5 feet long and as thick as my calf, we didn't know they got that big in this area. Unsure what it actually was, we debated for some time before we decided it was safe to jump!

One of the most legendary islands in Phang Nga Bay is nicknamed 'James Bond' Island since this was the site that the movie, 'Man With the Golden Gun' was filmed. It is a steep limestone protrusion which appears to have exploded out of the ocean and literally drips with implausible external stalactites covered in thick green vegetation.

Koh Hong, Thailand. Kendra, Brownyn (crew) and Graeme inside the inland lake of the hong.

Koh Phi Phi, Thailand. Long Tail Boats used for tours.

One of the many backpacker working crew
10 day 'visa run' trips from Thailand to Malaysia.

Chao Ley Sea Gypsies in Koh Phetra, Thailand.

Since you only get a 30 day visa in Thailand, you have to leave every month to re-new your visa - most yachts seem to see this as an annoyance and tend to hang around Malaysia instead, where you get a 2 month visa. We found it a great opportunity to compel us to explore new islands, hidden lagoons and to spend time in the crystal clear waters and abundant coral gardens you don't find that close to Phuket. Some of our favourite places are on the 'visa run', so we always looked forward to it!!!!

Islands on the 'visa' run
KOH LANTA, Muslim floating fishing village

Most people are familiar with the beaches on the West Coast of Lanta, but few visit the small Muslim floating fishing village on the south east corner of this Island. It is a really beautiful floating village, bursting with flowers and complete with inland banana plantations. The people are really gracious, and a walk through the village to buy a fresh chicken, the catch of the day (fish that is), or to just watch the children playing, can be most enlightening.

KOH MUK, the emerald cave and lost land of Jurassic Park

This is the most incredible Hong, accessed through a striking cave, given the name 'emerald cave' because of the way the sun reflects on the water inside the cave illuminating it and giving the appearance of 'glowing' bodies when you swim through it!!! The cave itself has amazing stalactites and stalagmites dripping from the ceiling and walls, iridescent apricots, greens, yellows and amber. The light is at its best when the sun is low (and the tourist has already gone home). Swim through the tunnel and as you approach the bend to the left everything goes utterly black - you cannot see your hand in front of your face - keep swimming!!!! Only a few seconds of darkness and then you see the bright light of the Hong right in front of you. Swim to the exit cave and welcome to the lost land of Jurassic Park - at least that's what it looks like!!! This enclosed lagoon has a white sand beach and gargantuan vegetation which belongs in a completely different era. The noise of the cicada (an insect that makes a shrill droning noise) inside this Hong echoes against the sheer walls giving a unique aura to the place and each plant has grown enormously, unspoilt by human intervention.

The first time we visited Koh Muk I was petrified about swimming in the pitch black, but one of our friends swam with me, holding my hand the whole way!

Another time we visited we jumped off the yacht into the sea to swim to the entrance, and swam into a mass of jelly fish spawn. They were not poisonous but it was like swimming through jelly, so was a very disconcerting experience.

KOH ROK NOK & NAI, home of Christmas tree worms

These are actually two islands, which you anchor in between. The water is crystal clear and the coral is quite diverse, particularly with strange polyps which reminded me of the little multi-coloured lemmings I used to display around my computer!!! They are actually called Christmas tree worms so the real name is just as good! They are all very vivid colours like orange, scarlet, neon blue and have little ornaments which make them twinkle!!! We usually get a really good deal from the fisherman here, last time landing a large bucket of tiger prawns, squid and 2 large coral trout for 100 baht!!!! (Less than $3).

KOH BULON, phosphorescent swimming at night
A small island with one very small bungalow development and not a lot else!!! Exquisite beaches, white sand and clear waters.

There is very little ambient light from the shore so it is a great place to go night snorkelling in the phosphorous - with no moon, the whole sea sparkles as you swim in the dark water - best to take a snorkel and swim in the stars!!!!! We have been known to 'speed snorkel' by dragging a rope behind the dinghy and holding onto it, whilst you snorkel in the sparkling water!!!!

KOH BUTANG - Tarautao National Marine Park

Koh Butang is a tiny island which doesn't seem to get any visitors, has no inhabitants, and has the most incredible coral gardens I have ever seen. The diversity of coral is the most varied I have seen in the Indian Ocean - I can only describe snorkelling off this island as soaring over a rich rain forest with visibility so clear you can see the forest floor itself. The coral is so high in places, with visibility up to 30m, that you feel you are viewing a mountain range, and every way you turn you discover a new plant, species or colourful fish. I was particularly in awe of the huge 'sunfish', shaped liked a giant multi-pointed starfish, which must have been three feet in diameter and neon blue and black.

Close to this island is **KOH LIPI**, which has a couple of small bungalow developments right on the beach, with a choice of 3 or 4 restaurants which put their tables on the white sand beaches to enable you to watch the sun go down and eat under the stars. It's a fine carefree tranquil island with clear water and dazzling white sand. You can take a walk over to the other side of the island and walk around the traditional Chao Ley village (sea gypsies) and watch them build wooden long-tail boats for fishing, and weaving traps or mending nets.

KOH ADANG, Home of Pirates Falls

This is the neighbouring island, and if you are energetic enough, can ascend a striking forest trail up to the precipice view point where you can see breathtaking views of the Butang Atoll. You can also take a different traill up to Pirates Falls - which used to be really beautiful until they dammed it to provide fresh water to KOH LIPI (That's progress for you). On the West coast, the beaches are pure white sand, absolutely bare accept for huge boulders which dominate the beach - they are quite spectacular to see and clamber over! The panorama here is very similar to the Similan Islands which are dominated by their gigantic boulders.

TARUTAO. The largest island of the 51 island national park archipelago.

 The densely forested, former penal colony has many walking trials leading to streams, pools and lookouts. The scenery is breathtaking in the rainforest, with many strangler vines hanging in twisted shapes. There are many species of wildlife, but this is the only place in Thailand we've come face to face with a large aggressive wild boar!!!!! The other islands, particularly the 'Butang' group, live up to their national park status, with stunning coral reefs which look like forests from the surface.

We once anchored here to be moved on by a large dinghy who claimed to be the film crew for a survival programme. They told us they had the authority of the Thailand government to ask yachts to move on if they thought we might provide temptation for the competitors on the island. We compromised and moved to an anchorage which was further from shore, but we did drag anchor because the anchorage was not as good. We guessed this island was remote enough to provide a good base for the television programme, especially since wild pig could be on the menu! I recently saw the third series of "Lost" and I swear this was the same beach used when "Jack" is in Thailand!

Koh Kradan is now known as the 'love' island since 18 couples got married under the water on Valentines Day. I'm not sure if this happens every Valentine's day, but the island seems to be quite famous for it now. The fish there were amazing and the little tiger fish constantly nibbled at your toes as you swam through huge schools of them. You were completely surrounded by all varieties of fish when you swam so it must have made a great scene for a wedding.

Koh Phetra – Bird Nest Island

Also known as 'bird nest' island, it is a very steep island with only one place to land your dinghy. We had heard that the sea gypsies (Chao Ley) that live here can be quite belligerent and territorial about their bird nests and that it is not recommended that you go ashore. The bird's nests are made from the spittle of birds high on the steep cliffs and the Chao Ley risk their life's to harvest the nests on a strict seasonal rotation so that the bird's continue to

78

nest there. The nests are sold as a delicacy and served as birds nest soup in high class restaurants. We did visit them on the island and they made us very welcome, showing us an example of the birds nest and trading a large fish for two packets of cigarettes. They did, however, make it quite clear that we should cook and eat the fish on the boat and not on the beach (this communicated with the help of sand drawings since we could not speak Thai and they could not speak English.)

Another money making opportunity

One of our priorities when we reached Thailand was to find a way we could make a living without compromising our life style. We had taken paying crew to Madagascar and for the Millennium in East Africa, so we decided we would use this as a model to design a life. There are many 'charter' companies in Thailand and Malaysia that offer luxury exploration of the many islands, providing state rooms with all the amenities you would expect in a hotel, maid service, and dining under the stars. These companies are all licensed by the Thai government and provide all the necessary insurance and health standards you would expect. We were not competing with these people, we were not even running a business (that would be illegal), we were simply inviting adventurous travellers to 'join in' with our lifestyle and experience everything we would experience.

As 'paying' crew, their contribution would pay for their food, bed, maintenance of the boat, diesel, propane and water. We built the cost to cover all expenses incurred and only did 10 day trips or more so that they could truly appreciate this way of life. They played a completely active part of the daily boating requirements, from helping to provision (we would go down to the market en masse and buy several weeks supply of fresh food) to cooking, cleaning, and boat maintenance. The only additional money we made on top of this was the later introduction of 'a bar' since we soon realised it wasn't practical for everyone to bring their own liquor aboard. We kept an 'honesty' tab and crew simply paid for what they drank.

Whenever a special occasion came up like Christmas or New Year we would invite friends to join us and pay as crew instead of spending their money on a package holiday. We often invited backpackers we met, but were always mindful to not compromise our way of life, after all, 10 days on a boat with relative strangers could turn out to be a disaster.

We joked that crew had to pass the 'test' before they were invited but neither of us could really define what the guidelines were; we just both had a sense for good people. I still email many of these 'crew' today, Philly and Dan from Ireland, Ronald and Cathy from South Africa, Ellen and Joyce from Holland, Kim from Vancouver, Glen from the US, Tom and Annabelle from London, we have all lived our separate lives for over 5 years, but still keep in contact.

Ronald and Cathy were inspired by our lifestyle and now get away when they can and hire a bare boat to cruise alone, Tom and Annabelle ended up buying a yacht in Thailand when they got off our boat and continued their travels on that yacht up the Red sea. Only a few weeks ago they sent me a funny story of their voyage back to the UK from Greece, via the French canals (they left their boat in storage there). So we touched people's lives showing them a different way to live. Christmas 2000 we decided to take a trip north close to the Burmese islands and with a mixture of 6 crew we experienced the unique islands of Surin and Similan.

The Surin Islands, Nomadic sea gypsies from Burma

This marine national park is the Thai island group closest to Burmese waters. Mostly uninhabited but for a few park rangers and nomadic sea gypsies. The Surin' consist of 2 main islands with off-lying islets and rocks with many sheltered anchorages. As with many of these Thai islands, you really need to be able to visit a few times with different weather conditions to truly appreciate all it has to offer. However, our first visit was over the Christmas period and we couldn't have chosen a more isolated paradise to celebrate. White sand beaches with the consistency of fine flour, turquoise clear waters and stunning coral gardens. On Christmas Eve we watched the sun set on a secluded beach with a fallen tree, bleached by sun, providing our 'cocktail seats'. I think it was so extraordinary just because we were the only people there to share a special moment in a truly beautiful place.

Koh Surin Nod – Christmas Day

Christmas day was spent in the larger bay of Koh Surin Nud with its glorious extensive white sand beach backed by abundant vegetation. A few locals challenged us to their version of 'hacky sack' played with a small hard weaved plastic ball and the only rules being you have to keep the ball in the air using your head, shins or forearm - they obviously don't bruise as easy as the 'farangs' , since we all found it pretty hard-going. Graeme returned from the yacht with home-made Pina Colada (coconut cream, fresh pineapple and Thai rum) which we sipped lying in the sea with our 'inflatable drinks-holder - a perfect day. Once the Christmas festivities were over we set sail south for the Similan Islands - reputed to be one of the top dive sites of the world - and therefore frequently visited by dive operators.

We had some of the best sailing we've experienced in Thai waters - a fairly consistent North Easterly wind blowing 20-25 knots, with the occasional gusts to 35 knots to add a little excitement!! Since Khulula is a heavy boat (20 tons) these are perfect conditions for her.

Similan Islands, one of the top dive sites in the world

This group of nine main islands with rocks and islets have derived their name from the Malay 'sembilan' meaning nine. The Islands are a popular dive site even though they lay 60 miles north of Phuket and can only be visited in the North East season (November-March). After the privacy of Surin we all felt a little 'crowded' when we arrived at Koh Similan and struggled to find a bit of solitude. However, the snorkelling definitely made up for this and we did manage to mostly avoid crowded waters. We found a small bay opposite the main anchorage on the most northern island (Koh Bangu) which turned out to be an exceptional snorkelling site first thing in the morning. Here the colossal boulders which litter the shorelines finely balanced on top of each other, also lie in chaotic heaps beneath the water to depths of 35 metres. Soft coral, tropical fish of every conceivable colour, pattern and size, create vast walls of colour which you swim through.

We moved further south to Koh Miang and found a lovely spot in turquoise waters backed by gigantic boulders. The water clarity was so clear it was difficult to believe that the depth sounder was showing 30ft and not trusting the instruments, I jumped in the water expecting to see the keel close to the bottom, but instead I was surrounded by thousands of brightly coloured fish suddenly attracted to the boat. I have never seen such a variety of fish in such a small space and the large trigger-fish with their strange bulging eyes that seem to be half-way down their bodies, seemed to be the leaders of the school. I shouted to everyone else to jump in and it really did feel like we were swimming in a very crowded aquarium. We spent 2 days exhausting ourselves with snorkelling before we moved further south to Koh Huyo, the most southern Island to celebrate New Years Eve.

Koh Huyo, New Years Eve 2001

It suddenly felt like we had returned to the Surin Islands - again we were on our own, and what a fantastic place to greet in 2002! The long white powdery beach was completely empty (4 miles of empty), fringed with palm trees and scattered boulders, it really was a picture postcard. As the evening progressed we were treated to the most magnificent moon-rise, the gigantic orange globe creeping out the water on the horizon. A sight not many had witnessed before. Before the moon rose higher, I urged everyone to jump in the inky black water with their snorkel and mask to witness the phosphorescence. The waters in Thailand are particularly good to see them on dark nights, but this night was particularly spectacular. I like to describe it through Philly's eyes because this was her first time - " It was like swimming through the stars, like millions of tiny fire-flies in the water" We all had great fun diving down and watching the glowing bodies as they disturbed the phospherescence.

Phuket – Vegetarian festival of body piercing

We had heard stories of the vegetarian festival that took place in Phuket town and decided to visit to see for ourselves. The festival is based on a religious fasting period where they are not allowed to eat meat or take part in any other gratification of the flesh in training for a meditative pageant of ghastly body mutilation. The theory is that the fasting and period of meditation allows the devotees to mutilate their bodies with large spikes and carry these spikes through the streets in procession, without experiencing any pain.

The grisly demonstration held no bounds to the imagination and many devotees had long spikes which went through one cheek, into the mouth, and out the other cheek, with attendees supporting the weight of the spike either ends, decorated with whole pineapples and watermelons. Other devotees used everyday items which they pierced through their faces such as a satellite dish, a child's bicycle and a flag pole! The most macabre sight was the self-mutilation by axe of the tongue where the devotee walked down the street with his tongue stuck straight out and carved it back and forth with the axe. His attendees tried to stem the flow of blood by constantly dabbing his chin and neck and yet his ceremonial apron was still soaked red. Another devotee used the axe in each hand which he then swung, to an imaginary drum beat, over his shoulders to take big slices of flesh out of his back.

I found the whole display quite distressing and I had to take sanctuary in one of the many food stands to take a cold drink and sit down before I fainted. I didn't return the following year to watch this festival or recommended that anyone else visited. This festival has nothing to do with Buddhism but has some strange significance in the animalistic religion and the power of mind.

Phuket – Songkran Festival

This festival is full of 'sanuk' which is the Thai word describing everything that is fun, enjoyable and that gives pleasure. It is a water festival which celebrates the coming of the rainy season and is celebrated by everyone throwing water over everyone else. During this time do not wear anything that you do not want to get wet in public because you are guaranteed to get water thrown over you. If you are riding a motorcycle down the street, someone will step off the kerb with a bucket of water and throw the whole bucket over you, if you are on a tuk tuk (which is like an open truck with 2 rows of seats), other people on the road will throw water into the tuk tuk. Even at the market everyone throws water around, with giant water pistols, buckets and even hose pipes! It is best to get into the spirit of things rather than avoid getting wet and it's best to just enjoy the chance to cool off in the hot climate!

Malaysia - Langkawi

This is a beautiful Island, very close to the Thai border and well worth a couple of days motorcycle hire. There are many stunning anchorages away from it all, at the North of the island (Hole in the wall) and surrounding islands. 'Hole in the wall' which is actually the Kisap River, on the North east coast of Langkawi, is so named because of the relatively narrow entrance to the mangrove forest from the ocean.

Once inside you can explore by dinghy the many branches of the mangroves. The various waterways lead to little known caves, home to bats which can be viewed at close range. Some of the caves have been enhanced to make access easier, whilst others seem less accessible. Exploring the mangroves in silence will reward you with spectacular sightings of fish eagles, brahminy kites, various 'monkeys' (watch out for the spectacled long-tail macaques as they forage for crabs), colourful kingfishers, hornbills and giant monitor lizards.

We were fortunate enough to watch an entire family of spectacled long-tail monkeys running across an old electric wire which was strung across the water. Despite shutting off our engine so we didn't startle the family, the monkeys panicked as they saw us below in the water and started to hastily scamper across the wire. It was a real scene to see the monkeys falling off the wire or catching themselves before they fell in the water with their long tails, but one mother was dangling by a hand and tail with a very small baby clutching her chest. We watched in dismay as the baby lost his grip and tumbled into the water below, screaming all the way. The mother instantaneously let go of the wire and dived into the water after her baby, and meantime the audience of the other monkey's on the shore were making an implausible racket pointing and screaming at the baby in the water. A large male launched himself into the water from the bank and started to swim anxiously towards the mother and baby, whilst the baby coughed and spluttered and swam to the family on the shore. I never even realised monkeys were such good swimmers, but they obviously don't choose to go in the water unless they have to!

We felt quite culpable that we had led to this catastrophe, but all the monkeys safely got to shore and then screamed at us from the trees for causing the calamity. Another example of how our presence can disrupt the delicate balance of nature.

Maidens Lake

Situated on Telok Dayang Bunting, this freshwater lake is reputed to be high in minerals and have healing qualities. Certainly after 10 days of saltwater, we're always pleased to see it!! Our clandestine access was via an old timber staircase which climbs the lowest point of the mountain and back down to the lake. It is certainly worth the exertion to have the solitude of this end of the lake, out of sight from the new 'tourist' jetty.

The emerald green lake is enclosed by steep jungle and the sounds of birds and frogs rebound off the water. Many monkeys can be spotted in the branches and they are quite used to the tourists who hand-feed them. You can also visit a catfish pond which is tightly packed with giant black catfish with their whiskers sticking out the water. The tourists are encouraged to sit on the edge of the pool and put their legs in water so that they can be tickled by the catfish as they swim around their legs (it's quite entertaining to watch everyone shrieking when they do this).

On the same island is an interesting cave accessed through the mangroves by foot. You can climb deep into the cavern through water, sometimes waist high and a little slippy! Graeme then explored further into the caves with the stronger members, to find the 3 large caverns accessible through hard climbing (and bat dodging!!!) Needless to say, I did not attempt this one!! Other anchorages on the surrounding islands provide tranquil beauty with steep rain forests, fantastic sunsets which light up the limestone outcrops, and plenty of sightings of giant fruit bats which erupt from the roof of the rainforests as the sun dips into the sea.

The ideal life?

We easily settled into life in Thailand and Malaysia. Every 6 weeks we did a visa run to Langkawi in Malaysia, taking paying crew, which were usually backpackers, and thus making enough money to maintain the boat, buy diesel and fuel for the dinghy, and buy food and drink. These were our only expenses since the boat was paid for, we did not stay in marinas but anchored for free, we had no insurance and provided our own electricity, refuse disposal and propane gas for cooking, hence we had no taxes or bills to pay.

It seemed that things couldn't get much better since we didn't want for money, Khulula provided a lovely home and we had a constant change of scenery and new guests to alleviate boredom.

Life was idyllic, or so I thought, until Graeme calmly announced one day that he didn't love me any more and would like me to leave the boat. My idyllic life suddenly fell apart and I was homeless, penniless, and jobless and stranded in Malaysia. Of course, this wasn't exactly the case, since Graeme wouldn't be so cruel as to force me to leave until I had decided where I was going, but my pride and a broken heart made me want to leave as quickly as possible.

James Bond Island, Phang Nga Bay, Phuket.

Chapter 6 - The second enlightenment

"When men come to like a sea life, they are not fit to live on land"
Samuel Johnson

Contemplation in Inland Malaysia and Northern Thailand

I had no idea what I should do, it had never occurred to me that I wouldn't be with Graeme for the rest of my life, living in Thailand and Malaysia or wherever Khulula happened to sail.

"Why don't you go backpacking?" asked Graeme. "It would do you good to be on your own for a change and it will give you time and space to decide what you want to do with your life"
It seemed very strange that my best friend was giving me advice how to cope with the break up of my lover (who happened to be the same person). No wonder I was so confused.
"Well, I guess I could try it for a short time and see how I like it; I could go to Penang first since we've been there before so at least it is familiar. I could go to the Cameron Highlands and visit the tea plantations that Kendra and Elizabeth told us about."

And so this was the beginning of my lone travel, in the hope that I would discover a new life, without my best friend, my great love or my loving home, Khulula.

It may appear I was taking this in my stride, which was the mask I was trying very hard to wear. My pride would not believe that this was really happening to me. I felt like I had been thrown overboard. I had sacrificed so much to go on this life journey with Graeme and now he was calmly announcing he wanted to continue it without me. It seemed like I was living in a movie set or something, this can not be real life. I have no where to go, I have no job, no home, no friends, no family and certainly no 'Plan B' and I'm in Malaysia.

My first trip alone to Penang was a very tearful one, as I watched Khulula disappearing at anchor as the ferry picked up speed. I had spent so much time living on a boat it was going to seem very strange sleeping on the land in strange beds. I'd always hated being alone and here I was more alone than I had ever been and suffering from a broken heart, with no friends or family for support.

I just swallowed back the tears and put myself on auto-pilot. I really had no choice. All I could think of was running away and escaping from the hurt I felt every time I looked at Graeme and Khulula.

As the ferry slowed down for the port of Penang I swallowed back the tears once more and put on my brave travelling face. Penang is a bustling multi-cultural town with a heavy English, East Indian and Malaysian influence. The streets have huge open drains where the giant rats dash in and out and garbage is strewn everywhere, Malaysians not being renowned for their cleanliness. The men always spit openly in the street and the pollution of the public buses is awful. Of course, I'd been here before with Graeme, so I knew to dodge the spit, open drains, rats and garbage, by walking on the road and avoiding the many hand-drawn rickshaws.

I headed for the main part of town my guide book advised was the 'backpackers' area, and secured a single bed-bug ridden cot in a dark small room with no windows (on Love Lane!) Pretty different from the boat, I'm telling you.

This was obviously not the place to be when I was feeling lonely and sad, even though I tried for a few days to visit the local temples and attractions alone. I sat most of the time with my head buried in the guide-book drinking cold beer, chain-smoking and trying to figure out this back-packing game. I decided to head for the cooler mountains of the Cameron Highlands and the famous English tea plantations. It was pretty simple to arrange the bus once I decided to go there, and the following morning my transfer taxi was waiting to take me to meet it.

As soon as the bus started to wind through the mountains I immediately felt better and started chatting with some of the locals on the bus. Once I arrived at my destination I headed for the backpacking lodge I had chosen from the guide-book and started to explore the area. I was surprised how many single travellers there were, so I quickly started conversations and didn't feel so lonely. I was actually a bit of a novelty, since most were gap year travellers a good ten years younger than me, so they liked my stories of living on a sail boat (as I did). I even met a lone female traveller from California a few years older than me, so we joined up to visit the tea plantations together.

One of the many temples in Penang, Malaysia

One of the ideas I had was to find a new career, but my heart wasn't really in it and I was just marking time. I walked the hotels and hostels in the Cameron Highlands, hoping to secure a job in this breathtaking area with its wonderful climate of cooler mountain air and the rich green fields of tea. I loved the locality with its multi-cultural Indian and Malaysian food, dense rain forest jungle, and fun backpackers. I soon discovered though, it was not that easy to work in a foreign country without a work permit despite the heavy English influence in this area.

That first trip lasted three weeks before I rang Graeme from a phone box and begged to return and discuss our future. I just wouldn't believe this is what he really wanted and secretly hoped he had missed me. It became apparent though that Graeme wanted a permanent split and so I planned to make the most of a bad situation by returning to Khulula and packing a bigger backpack to visit all the inland destinations I heard all our backpackers discussing when they were aboard Khulula.

I had never travelled alone and that short trip had shown me it wasn't so bad, it was the best plan I could come up with until I figured something else out anyway. I needed some kind of distraction to stop the constant tears and heaving of my heart, staying close to Khulula was not the answer because that hurt

89

even more. I wanted to prove to Graeme I would not be beat, I was strong and I would survive without him. The short term plan was to visit inland Malaysia, Northern Thailand and then continue to Lao and Cambodia. I had no time scale and limited funds; I just hoped that at the end of this time I would have a new life plan.

The only thing I knew for sure was that I could not return to England to live with my Mum and Dad to listen to them say ' I told you so.' It would be like returning home with my tail between my legs.

I headed across the country to the Taman Negara National Park and decided to take a 3 day hike into the jungle. The Malaysian guide, Bok, assured me he would help me out if I struggled with my back and even lent me some sturdy hiking boots (which another backpacker had left behind).

I set off with two other backpackers who were going on the same trip - Martine from Singapore and Anya from Germany, two other lone female travellers. I was soon to realise that single travellers always tend to join up so that you're never really travelling alone.

On the way to the jungle in Bok's car, we stopped at Lata Rek and cooled down in the cool waterfall, before arriving at the jungle base camp, where we prepared for the first trek to the animal hide. Bok set off in the lead, carrying everyone's camping gear and food, whilst the three girls followed behind. I was almost surprised that he kept his bargain seeing as he was quite a large lad with plenty of extra weight, not the usual hiking guide image you might imagine. He was a jolly fellow though, happily walking along at a good pace loaded down with all our packs and telling us all about the National Park and the local hill tribe people of this area.

Diary excerpt: Beware jungle leeches

Thank god for the socks I bought and the wise move to tuck my trousers into those socks! Thank god for the hiking boots that Bok provided, hiking in my reefer sandals would have invited the leeches to a party! Martine picked up a nice big leech which was burrowing itself inside her skin and we were all aghast at the sight.

Bok reacted hastily and grabbed the leech by the tail, just before it disappeared; it was frantically trying to burrow its way under her skin. He then took the cigarette out of his mouth he was smoking and burnt the end of the tail of the leech, which instantaneously let go. First lesson of the jungle.

We arrived at the basic hide which had a number of cots and an open wall at one end (where you were supposed to spot the animals). Bok announced we were going on an evening hike through the jungle, which I quickly declined (being terrified of leeches you couldn't see and the dark!). This meant I had to stay behind alone, but I still preferred this option to trekking out there in the pitch black! My heart was pounding watching them disappear into the jungle, each with a small flashlight. I was left alone in the hide and was instantaneously bombarded by giant insects attracted to my candle light; I shone the light around and spotted giant ants large enough to carry you away! The giant black ants are honey ants and have large honey sacks on their backs; Bok says they are very tasty, so I decided not to be intimidated by them. They must have felt way more scared of me.

Since I'm alone, I'm overwhelmed by the sounds of the jungle. So many diverse songs of insects, frogs and birds, all in competition for the loudest sound! Despite the 'jungle deet' I'm definitely being eaten alive and it's really hot and humid. I'm sweating like a pig and although it's 8.30 p.m. it feels hotter than it did in the day.

Now it's really dark and I mean BLACK, and the girls are out there somewhere. I'm just watching a striking moth which I mistook for a small bird because of the size, and it keeps rebounding off the ceiling, spellbound by my candlelight. It is so large that it makes a reverberation like a hammer and when I shine my flash light onto it, it glows bright orange near the mouth but has a pure white furry body, but quite plain brown wings. It must be at least 12 inches across in size. There is a really adorable frog on the wall which makes an exquisite sound and I remember from the exhibition at the base camp that this is a flying frog. I have never felt so aware of nature, I don't seem to be afraid of the dark anymore.

Bok left something cooking on the camp stove and it smells appetizing, surely they should be back by now? It's almost 9.00 p.m. now so they've been gone more than an hour, I wonder if they got lost? They said they were only going for a 20 minute walk to try and spot the phosphorescent mushrooms and any night animals around and I'm beginning to feel a little concerned. One and a half hours later, two very exhausted girls trampled back to the hide clutching the glowing mushrooms in their hands, which really were quite spectacular, glowing bright orange and yellow. They said they looked miraculous on the jungle floor. I was still glad I didn't go; they both said they were worried about the leeches and the walk was much longer than they anticipated. Martine had borrowed a pair of my socks so she could tuck her trousers into them and she said she was really glad she did it since it was too dark to spot any of the little monsters.

This morning we had a lovely walk over a suspended rope bridge which hung thirty metres (about 90 feet) in the air from the canopy floor. It was not a place for anyone who suffered vertigo to be, particularly as it swung considerably as you walked on it. I loved to see the jungle from this height, viewing the tops of trees, instead of the trunks, and watching the colossal bee hives which hung from the tree tops, their honey-combed plates buzzing with activity.

The tallest tree in the Malay Peninsular is called Tualang, and stands at 173 metres tall (that's over 500 feet tall) and exists in this variety of rain forest jungle. I was looking at trees 60 metres tall (180 feet) and that seemed really imposing from where I was standing. (see the picture opposite and note the rope bridge is tied close to the top of one of these tall trees).

The tree only flowers once every 10 years, and they lose all their leaves, all at once, every year. Regrettably because of the infrequent flowering, the tree is now threatened with extinction since it was established in a cooler climate, which is now considerably warmer (the last ice age did not effect the Peninsular but did lower the temperature). The base of the tree has high buttresses for support because their root systems are not deep; so many old trees are rotten and hollow inside.

An enchanting, if short, river trip was another highlight, although our canoe struggled up stream against the small rapids. Bok skilfully steered us to a natural gravel sand bank which created a deep water pool we could bathe in. After making camp and building a fire, the girls set to making dinner over the camp fire. The fishing was unsuccessful, so Anja and Martine created what they could with the dry ingredients that Bok carried. He had set up a small tent for us all to sleep in, but it had the effect of creating a greenhouse, so Anja opted to sleep in her sleeping bag by the fire on the beach, whilst Martine opted for the hammock, strung up across two trees.

Suspended rope bridge with Anja & Martine, Taman Negara National Rainforest

Cameron Highland Hilltribe village children, Malaysia

Tea plantation, Cameron Highlands, Malaysia

I opted for the tent, which was not very comfortable since I had to lie on the hard ground (I didn't think to bring a sleeping mat), and use my backpack as a pillow. By the morning a swarm of bees wanted to make my tent into their new hive and it was quite a dash to open the flap and escape before they swarmed inside. Apparently, it was the honey season and lots of bees were around and the constant buzzing was really irritating (as opposed to terrifying which I used to be of bees, again accepting nature banished another of my previous fears). I didn't let them stop me performing my morning duties, and after I had dug a hole for a make shift toilet, I took a cool shower in the river.

For our return journey back to the base camp we built rafts out of bamboo poles and drifted in the current down the river. I got the impression the poles had already been trimmed and cut to the exact size required, so all we really did was tie them together. It was a wonderful way though to complete our trip into the jungle.

The Perenthian Islands, snorkelling guide extraordinaire

From here I continued across to the East coast and caught a ferry to the Perenthian islands. I walked the beach with my heavy pack looking for accommodation that I could afford and soon discovered many backpackers worked on this island in exchange for accommodation and food (and sometimes tips). Without too much trouble I secured myself a job as a customer service co-ordinator for a small resort which catered to Kuala Lumpans on 4 day trips from the city. The deal was that I got free accommodation and food in return for greeting guests and organising any leisure activities for them.

After a couple of weeks I also became the snorkelling guide (which I discovered was for parties of 40 plus non-swimmers!) and the work load started to get really hefty considering I was getting no pay! I brought in another couple of backpackers to help me (on the same deal) but it became apparent pretty quickly we were being taken for a ride. It was nice to stay in an air-conditioned room, but the food was not that good and we hardly got any spare time to benefit from our environment.

One thing I did get a lot of pleasure from was watching the giant monitors which visited the kitchens everyday to be fed scraps. These crocodile-like lizards must have been six feet long and it was fascinating to watch them eat the scraps from the safety of my balcony! I often escorted guests across to the other side of the island and saw many of these giant monsters lying in the shade of a tree or under a hut (which I would point out to them as tour guide extraordinaire).

On the way over to the other side of the island you had to walk through an area of dense jungle where the trees overhung the path forming a kind of ceiling and if you looked up into the ceiling you would see giant black spiders hanging from their webs just above your head. You would hear women backpackers screaming who were happily walking down the path but not looking up until someone pointed upwards (usually when they were half way down the path so that they couldn't quickly escape). It was always fun to point them out to my guests as part of the tour of the island.

I plead to be urinated on

The job came to end when I had an accident on one of the snorkeling trips which alerted me to how badly organised this resort was. I was accountable for over 40 non-swimmers (and I'm not such a strong swimmer myself and have no life-saving skills) and we were trying to track a couple of giant sea turtles. We spotted the turtles and I jumped in the water to follow them whilst the boats with the other snorkelers followed me so everyone else could jump in and watch the turtles. I was so intent on following the turtles under water that I didn't realise I'd swam into a giant pod of jelly fish. I was completely covered in the finger-sized jelly fish which immediately injected me with their toxin. As I thrashed in the water to try and get the jelly fish off me which had stuck to my skin all over my face and neck, a boat picked me up and dragged me out the water (not my boat, but one from another resort).

No one had vinegar (which immediately neutralises the toxin) so I was shouting for anyone to urinate on me (which has the same effect), which no one would. In the meantime I was going into shock and imploring someone to urinate in a jar or container so I could use it to neutralise the toxin. Everyone was too embarrassed to help me and didn't realise how ill I could be. All they would do is drop me at the nearest resort to try and seek medical help, which is what they did. At the resort no one knew what to do and so I asked for directions to the kitchen and shouted for vinegar. Eventually they understood what I wanted to do with the vinegar when I explained to them how it neutralises the toxin. It took me over a week to recuperate from the welts which were left all over my face and body, and this is when I decided it wasn't worth the pay! I'd spent enough time on the islands anyway, so I decided this was a good opportunity to force myself to move on.

Even though I was now on the East coast of Malaysia, it wasn't that far to enter Northern Thailand via Hat Yai. In fact, it seemed quite common for people to take this route so I wasn't short of other lone backpackers for company.

Diary excerpt:
As I left Malaysia I made a note to remember how helpful the muslim men were when they saw me struggling with my

backpack. In Thailand though, you don't even have to struggle because they actually anticipate that you need help! Back in the 'Land of Smiles' I stepped off the ferry at Saturn and saw a big welcoming sign 'Welcome to Thailand' with the small words underneath (except drug traffickers) which always bought a little smile to my face. I always wondered if thieves and murderers were therefore welcome too…

I didn't need to worry about how I was going to get to Hat Yai or carry my heavy backpack I couldn't actually carry alone. As I dragged them off the ferry, I dumped them, knowing they would be safe, and went to check in with immigration. A motorbike taxi approached me and asked in broken English

"Where you go?" "To Hat Yai" I reply

"No problem, I take you to bus", and with that he grabbed my large back pack and grinned at the surprising weight, as he launched it onto his shoulders and led me to his 100cc moped. He somehow balanced the huge bag between his knees resting his chin on the top of the pack so he could see the road, and I delicately sat side-saddle with my other bag on my knee. You must ride side-saddle as a female wearing a skirt and it is very impolite to stride the pillion of a motorbike taxi, so I had become quite an expert at the art.

Both of us finely balanced we trundle off for the 20 minute ride which cost less than a dollar. He chats along in his broken English, asking me questions, as my legs, which are dangling with no foot support, begin to numb. He takes me to the mini-bus stop and unloads my big pack pointing to the mini-bus which is just about to leave. My timing is really tight and they won't let me on that bus because my bag is too big and the last seat has just been sold. I am devastated. I'm in the middle of nowhere, my only friend, the motorbike taxi, has already left, and if I miss my connection for the train I miss the night train I was planning for my overnight accommodation. I plead and I beg, not realising all the seats have been sold, until a Thai lady steps forward and hands me her ticket. I am amazed. She just smiles at me and says "Take ticket, I wait, you miss train" I carefully put my two hands together and make a low bow, the traditional thanks which also shows her I understand she is making merit. (Do you think someone in Canada or America or England would do that?)

I get to the train station with 10 minutes to spare and there is a queue at the ticket booth. A couple of western girls turn to me and tell me the train is booked solid for Bangkok for the next 3 days. NEXT 3 DAYS!! I approach the ticket booth and pray they can somehow squeeze me in. They have one, 1st class ticket available only and I don't have enough cash to pay for that (it's double the cost of the 2nd class ticket). I quickly look at the 2 western girls and ask them if there is an ATM nearby, and yes, there is. I leave my bags where they are and run to the ATM machine to get more cash, it will cost me more than that to stay in Hat Yai for 3 days so it's worth it. By the time I return, the ticket lady has already instructed a guard to put my bags on the train and she quickly takes my money, pointing at the guard who's running down the platform with my bags! I follow him and he directly takes me to my first class carriage. You don't tip Thaïs; they are insulted by it because they are doing their best for you anyway to make merit, which is much more important.

I've paid for first class, so I have high expectations. When I'm shown the cabin, I smile to find a young Thai woman with a sick baby covered in spots (oh no!!!). I go and get some fresh air and chat with the conductor who tells me all about his family and then questions me where my husband is? How many children do I have? How old am I? We chat about Buddhism and he is soon placing his hand on my thigh and planning an evening of Thai whiskey on the train! I'm given coffee, invited to share his dinner and learn all there is to know about this 62 year old conductor! As he gets increasingly friendly, I decide it is a good time to retire to my cabin (with a lock) for a short rest! I head for the dining car, dodging all the Thai's gambling and laughing and realise even the 2nd class carriages are really loud tonight. It's probably a good thing I'm in the private first class carriage, even though I'm sharing it with a spotty baby! At least I'll get some sleep! (Thai babies do not cry, not even when they are ill, babies only cry for attention).

9.30 a.m. Everyone has been on the train now for 15 hours, some more. The gambling games are still going on, getting more frantic, the bids higher and higher and some carriages are completely blocked by a game going on around a table with everyone crowded around. I quickly count over 1000 baht(approx $20 US) on a table, so the stakes are now high, but everyone is still smiling and laughing and covering their tables with shared snacks of sunflower seeds and monkey nuts.

I was using an old 'Rough Guide to Asia' to plan my travelling and I set myself a budget of $10 US dollars per day (Including accommodation, travelling and food). This was quite feasible if you stayed in the cheapest huts and ate street food from the stalls. The Rough Guide gave you a good selection of this price-range accommodation. It was also a guaranteed way of meeting like-minded backpackers because they would be staying in the same places.

I became to love the Thai railway system and found it extraordinarily economical and comfortable and second class accommodation usually gave you a restful sleeping berth for the long journeys, saving on a night's accommodation at either end of your destination. In fact, it was an experience in itself watching the porters make up your berth with crisp white sheets and pillowcases.

On the first train journey I took, I walked down the cars whilst my porter was making up my berth. I was inquisitive about the non-sleeping cars in 3rd class, and I found a deafening, confused tone of hilarity and cheer and could hardly pass down the corridors where crowds of Thai people were teeming around several tables where ferocious gambling was taking place. It was quite astonishing to see such a good-tempered ambience when so much money was swapping hands; piles of the distinctive pink 500 baht note randomly thrown on the tables. The Thai people do like to gamble and spend lots of money on the national lottery, but as always, do it with a smile and geniality. I was glad I had opted for the 2nd class carriage with the sleeping berths, and returned to a quiet atmosphere of Thai families and travellers settling down for a good nights sleep. Obviously, if the train is full, it is wiser to book the private 1st class carriages!

The starting point to explore Northern Thailand was Bangkok, and from here I decided to visit Kanchanaburi and the Bridge of the River Kwai which was only two hours by bus.

Kanchanaburi and the bridge over the River Kwai

Although many people visit for the historical tale of the bridge over the River Kwai, the surrounding countryside had much to offer, so I decided to take a tour with Toi's Tour for around 550 baht ($10

99

US), which was a fun trip in an air-conditioned mini bus and a safe driver.

Elephant ride through the jungle

The first stop was the elephant camp for a 45-minute ride aboard a bamboo chair mounted on the elephant. They carefully select the weight of passengers to the size and age of the elephant and treat their animals with great respect. I was riding with Michaela, from Jersey, and we ended up with the smallest youngest elephant with a BIG personality. We giggled as the Mahout (elephant trainer) was trying to convince our elephant to walk through mud. He simply didn't want to get his feet muddy and always screeched to a halt whenever we approached a muddy puddle. As we ambled towards the river, the incline was steep and it was quite difficult to hold onto the back of the chair to prevent your body from falling forwards, but our elephant appeared to be in a rush to wash his muddy feet in the river.
The ride seemed longer than 45 minutes and very enjoyable. We clambered off our elephant onto a bamboo platform and headed to the river to do some river rafting before we visited the waterfall.

Sai Yok Noi Waterfall

Next stop Sai Yok Noi waterfall, one of the most impressive I have seen in South East Asia, set in lush jungle and cascading from a great height, forming strong falls of water which you can bathe under. I was one of the first to clamber up the rocks to stand right underneath the torrents of water cascading down and experience the cold water pounding my body. It is quite unusual to be able to get so close to the falls and this is why this place is so special. This is maybe one of the first places I understood my oneness with nature and didn't feel lonely. Maybe this travelling alone was good for me afterall.

Hin Dat hot springs

A short stop for lunch before heading for Hin Dat hot springs. As you cross the river you get the first sight of two steaming pools set in a tropical jungle; an exquisite paradise waiting to be sampled. We are instructed to first take a dip in the chilly river before plunging into the first natural hot spring pool that maintains a constant temperature of 35oc. After 15 minutes you then climb into the second pool which is 20oc hotter, which at 55c is like a hot steaming bath, and then repeat the process at least 3 times. This very therapeutic experience left you feeling exhilarated and rejuvenated for the final part of our day trip to visit the 'Death Railway'.

Hin Dat hot springs

The Death Railway

The 257 mile long Thailand-Burma railway started construction in June 1942 and was planned to be the crucial link between Japan's newly acquired territories in Singapore and Burma. With an almost impenetrable terrain and only basic picks and shovels it was responsible for 16,000 POWs and 100,000 Asian labourers' deaths by the time it was completed 15 months later. Thirty-eight Prisoners of War (POW's) died for each mile of track laid and so it was nicknamed 'the Death Railway'. The railway is very scenic and the short train journey takes you through a ninety-foot solid rock cutting at Wang sing and the Wang Po viaduct, where a trestle bridge nearly a thousand feet long clings to the cliff face as it curves with the River Kwai Noi. The thrill of hanging out the windows as the train slowly crosses the viaduct feels a little like a helter skelter ride as you stare down into the abyss below.

The following day I attended the 'Festival of Light' which celebrated the anniversary of the destruction of the Bridge over the River Kwai and I watched as an open air theatre group of more than 200 performers re-enacted the story of the POW's, with the help of old news footage showing the actual events projected onto a giant screen of water across the river. It seemed amazing that I was watching a spectacular light and water show in this part of the world, complete with translation head phones so I could hear the story in English. The light and sound spectacular featured some of the latest computer generated technology with four dimensional speakers and pyrotechnics including more than 2,000 fireworks. The event concluded with a spectacular fireworks display which mimicked planes bombing the bridge and destroying it. It was really well choreographed with life-like explosions and bombs falling from the air, leaving the bridge shrouded in smoke.

The cottages I stayed at were set in beautiful gardens, with the more expensive cottages right on the river front, but I was still within my $10 a day budget (although the trip obviously exceeded that). From here I decided I wanted to head further North, so I returned to Bangkok to catch the overnight train for Chaing Mai and the Northern territories of Thailand.

The little town of Pai and sleeping in the garlic fields

I had heard a lot about the mountain area of Pai and decided to take the two hour mini-bus trip from Chaing Mai into that area. It certainly turned out to be an especially peaceful and reflective place and I slept the first night in a very rudimentary bamboo hut deep in the garlic fields. With no electricity or water and a dreadfully simple mattress, this was one of the cheapest and most humbling experiences I had so far. The following morning I could hear the quiet, the river flowing, the low mumble of farmers planting garlic, the birds, insects and frogs. I set off back to the main area for a shower and breakfast and spent over an hour trying to navigate myself across the fields. Looking over the land each group of bamboo huts look identical, it was impossible to tell which group belonged to the farmers, and which have been adapted for the tourists with hot water, showers, and electricity. I stopped to ask the Thai farmers directions and they just laughed and waved in their normal polite manner, directing me to nowhere in particular! That is a lesson you need to learn in Thailand, the people would lose face if they refused help or was not able to help a stranger, so it is better for them to point you somewhere so you appear to be grateful and satisfied. This can mean often that you end up more lost than you were before you asked for help (as was in my case since they pointed me to a road which ended up quite a distance from the huts I was staying), but they gave you help which means they have made merit.

This is also known as 'Kreng Jai' or 'Awe Heart' which is sometimes translated as 'consideration' or 'deference' but neither of these words do justice to the connotations of Kreng Jai; if one is in 'awe' of others feelings this carries with it an implicit obligation to respect others' feelings. This involves two aspects, the first of which is to avoid imposing on other people, and the second of which is to avoid confrontations which suggest dissent. The farmers felt this obligation to respect my feelings and avoid confrontation by providing a solution to me; if they had just shrugged and ignored me they could have possibly incited a confrontation. Kreng Jai is a unique form of Thai behaviour which is also influenced by respect and obedience to elders, trust in their wisdom and protection, and the need to return favours received. The underlying idea is the principle of mutual dependence and reciprocity, and the principle of being practically and morally indebted. It is the recognition that people need each other if they want to go on living. Behaviour is also influenced by respect or fear of the powerful, respect for superiors and consideration for foreigners (mostly because they are an unknown quantity).

Once you start to spend some time around the Thai people you begin to understand this philosophy more and it is very evident around families who obviously mutually respect and consider one another. Even to the small child who is never ignored as you see in the Western world. Indeed, the very notion of pushing a child in a pushchair in front of the parents would be unacceptable since the child is dependable on the parent (and the child is quite alone in the front this way.) This is why you rarely see Thai babies or children cry, the whole extended family give one another mutual support rather than using outside services such as kindergarten or nurseries. If a woman has to work, her mother or her sister or even her cousin may take care of the child. In turn, the child is taught respect for superiors and so the western 'tantrum' you see so much in the Western world, is also absent here. A child is never put in front of a T.V. or a computer game to occupy it because the parent does not have time. The child 'joins in' with every daily activity, observing mother folding the laundry or riding on the back of a farmer woman.

The whole philosophy of life in Thailand is so different from the Western world.

The tranquil mountains of Pai

Diary excerpt:

The mist lifting from the mountains in the early morning light has a peaceful effect on body and mind. Everyone feels relaxed and tranquil in this environment.

Heidi is peacefully playing her guitar crossed-legged on the bamboo floor overlooking the River Pai; she has discovered her passion for music. Everyone gets a chance to reflect on life here, so it should be a good place for me to stay a while.

That is one of the great things about Pai; you can choose how close you want to be to the locals' way of living. Right next to the huts I am staying in are the beautiful Rim Pai cottages, with individual hardwood huts nestled in the trees with their own private balconies overlooking the river. This is where you'll find ensuite tiled bathrooms with flushing western toilets and comfortable beds (and still only for $25 a day). Personally, I'd choose the bamboo hut with shared toilets and a simple shower any day. Hot water is supplied by electric heaters, which is most common, but I did see a giant cauldron heated by coals - a novel way to bathe in the open-roofed showering hut. Scooping the boiling water into a bucket would certainly involve some careful mixing with cold water before tipping it over your head!

Diary excerpt:

The mist has almost completely lifted from the mountains now, exposing a bright blue sky and a bright warm sun, with a chill still in the air. I'm here in December, which is one of the best times to visit Northern Thailand, with warm sunny days and cool nights and mornings. Late November to February is the cool season, and March to May the hot season, so I ended up here at the right time.

Exploring the area was easy and convenient; you choose how much you want to spend and how you get around. The simplest and cheapest way is by motorbike for around 150 baht (approx

$4US) a day with insurance. If you don't fancy doing it alone there are always plenty of other travellers you can join in with for the day. If your time is limited or you want to visit with a guide, choose from many of the tour companies offering everything from a 5-day trek across the mountains, staying each night in a different hill tribe village, to an elephant trek which ambles through the local jungle. I was lucky enough to meet up with a group of other backpackers who shared the cost of motorbikes, so I rode pillion passenger with one of them. Most of the single travellers I met were on a tight budget so there never seemed to be a shortage of people asking around to share costs. I often wondered how different this travelling experience would have been if I had a limitless supply of money to spend on accommodation and excursions. I suspect the experience would not be as "rich" as the one I was having.

If you simply fancy drifting down the river, many of the guesthouses supply giant rubber tires or choose a simple bamboo raft - either way, be prepared to get wet in the chilly water. Pai Adventure rafting take organized trips which is a safer option given some of the dangerous currents and fast overflows. I got hours of entertainment watching other backpackers getting dunked in the fast flowing brown water, sitting on the balcony and sipping cold beer. For a truly relaxing experience, visit one of the many natural hot spas or stay a few days at the natural hot spring bungalows or Thai Pai spa camping. If you feel tired from an exhausting day of clambering through giant caves and visiting waterfalls, opt for a traditional Thai massage, or book yourself onto a course and learn how to do it yourself!

There is so much available in Pai to keep you occupied (learn Thai cooking, reflexology, reiki course or yoga); you could forget to simply relax and enjoy the special ambience and beauty of this wonderful place. The huts I was staying at often ran unpretentious Thai cooking classes where a group of backpackers stood around a couple of Thai girls who shared their secrets. I still cook some of my favourite authentic Thai dishes from a hand-made recipe book written by one of the Thai girls and translated by a back-packer.

I also attended modest yoga classes which were held on the high balcony of the restaurant by a backpacker who made money for her travelling by asking for donations (which she got plenty of).

She easily made enough money for accommodation and food and beer and probably enough for travelling too, since most people donated a few dollars a session and she attracted around 20 people per session. I did wonder if I could come up with a money making activity like this so I could just keep travelling and live like this as long as possible (maybe I should write a book?).

The hill tribe people of Northern Thailand

One of my motorbike trips to explore the area took us to visit a remote village tribe of Karen long necks. I was very humbled by this experience and felt really privileged to meet and talk with the tribal women. The villages of Northern Thailand's mountain people are home to a number of distinct ethnic groups, the main ones being Karen, Hmong, Lahu, Yao and Lisu. There are approximately 300,000 Karen in Thailand, making them the most populous minority group. They have lived in the area far longer than any other mountain people, perhaps 200 years or more and originated from neighbouring Burma (now called Myanmar), home to more than 4 million Karen. The Karen Hill tribe can be divided into several sub-groups, the largest of which are the *sgaw karen* and *pwo karen*. The long-neck tribe is called Padung and are divided into 2 societies called Ee-lu-phu and kai-ph. I could not ascertain which society wore the brass rings and which stretched their earlobes with giant rings, but it was very evident in the village that 2 societies existed. The children of both societies were in mixed classes and were being taught English as well as their traditional language and customs.

'Long Necks' result from wearing many bronze rings around their necks from age 5

Members of the society who wear many tight bronze rings around their necks are initiated from the age of 5, with the rings being added 5 at a time by being 'coiled' around their necks and tightened. Another coil is added every several years until the age of 16. The woman I was talking to was carrying 11 pounds of rings on her neck, and wears them constantly. They clean them daily with lemon juice and wear cloth around the chin area to prevent chafing. They also wear one set of rings on their calves and one girl was suffering from water retention, causing considerable chafing. The pressure of the weight of the brass actually squashes the collarbones and ribs, and to remove a full stack would cause collapse of the neck and suffocation. They are proud to be carrying on the tradition, although there is no head-man pressure to do so. Women not wearing the rings are a small percentage, but are evident.

The Padung tribe are famous for producing the best *mahouts* (elephant handlers), and many mahouts grow up with the elephant they are assigned. It is not uncommon for the elephant to be the same age as the mahout and the elephant is very much part of the family. Many of the women weave scarves and wall hangings to provide funds for the village for education for the children and village medical supplies. Prior to the intervention of the Thai government, their traditional cash crop was opium. The government intervened with big incentives to encourage more legal cash crops and handicrafts. The girls I talked to were weaving and selling their handicrafts, and seemed very warm and friendly with big smiles and were eager to practice their English. I hope their culture and traditions will not be affected too much by the western tourists who visit, but it does appear to be controlled by the simple fact they are difficult to reach.

After a few weeks it was time to move on again and I headed back to Chaing Mai, via mini-bus, to visit a silk factory where you could see the silk being made from the silk-worm right through to the dying and weaving of the silk. It was a very educational and informative experience, and very relevant knowledge for Thailand, so it seems only fair I should pass this knowledge on here.

How is silk made?

The silk worm goes through 7 stages of its life cycle before it hatches into a butterfly. The first stage, which is the "egg stage," lasts 10-12 days before hatching into tiny worms which progress to small maggot-sized worms within 5-6 days. By stage 5 the worms resemble caterpillars and grow for a further 7-8 days, feeding on mulberry leaves, before commencing the weaving of their own cocoons in preparation for transformation. The cocoons takes 9-10 days to complete and the progress is monitored closely to pick the optimum time to terminate the natural life cycle of the worm by exposing it to light.

The cocoons resemble small oval marbles of yellow fibrous material - about the same size as an almond for Thai silk.

107

Japanese silk cocoons are around the same size but slightly rounder and white in appearance. The cocoons are harvested by placing 20-30 in boiling water to soften the fibre so the first yarn can be identified. Each cocoon will harvest between 800 - 1000 meters and are hand spun to uncoil.

Once the yarn has been processed, it is ready for dying in giant vats, the many beautiful colours achieved by carefully mixing the dyes accordingly, and for the more complex designs alternating different colours across a single yarn. The yarns are then dried naturally in the sun on giant frames. Once dyed, the yarn is hand-spun from bamboo spools and either coiled further onto smaller spools ready for the weaving machine, or hand stretched across giant frames ready for the basic framework of the weaving machine. Setting up a weaving machine takes a whole day, and as many as 120 rolls are hand stretched in the right combinations of colours to achieve the desired colour or design. It takes 4000 individually threaded yarns to make the basic framework for the machine set-up and each cycle of the bamboo weaving frame can weave just 200 meters of cloth. The weavers work 10 hours a day and in that time complete only 8 to 9 meters, depending on their skill. It is not surprising therefore, that Thai silk holds such a prized reputation throughout the world for its quality and wondrous colours. Modern fabrics have tried to simulate the feel and texture of 100% Thai silk, but the real thing is not that difficult to recognize if laid side by side. However, if you really want to test the theory you can do a simple 'burn' test to ascertain if it is the real thing by holding a lighter to the fabric and allowing it to burn. If it is 100% silk it will not burn and it will smell of human hair as the flame extinguishes itself. If it is artificial silk, the flame will continue to burn and the fabric will smell like melted plastic.

Thai silk is available in 3 different ply's according to its end use:
1 ply is generally used for shirts/blouses/skirts and scarves
2 ply is for dresses, jackets and trousers
4 ply is for suits and upholstery
The price of silk directly relates to how many yarns are used to achieve the thickness required and the labour required weaving either plain, mixed or patterned designs.

Chiang Mai, the city for the Hill tribes

Chiang Mai is a beautiful city and Thai women can be seen busy on the streets everyday cleaning the streets with a simple grass brush and a pan. It must be very satisfying work for them since they seem to have a constant smile on their face. The construction workers also seem to enjoy their work. Women as well as men laugh and sing whilst they toll in the mid-day heat, dressed in many layers to protect them from the sun and the dust.

The gas station is usually only visited by motorbikes, since this is the main form of transport in most of Thailand, and gas is sold by the bottle (usually a Sangsom whiskey bottle) because that's the only way to measure out of the larger drum.

The evening market in Chiang Mai is a colourful and cultural event, a chance for many of the hill tribe women to sell their crafts and the local farmers to sell their produce. As usual the sight of fresh meat sold in the sun with no refrigeration takes some getting used to, but it still doesn't stop you from tasting the many barbecues and snack stalls which line the street with delicious Thai delicacies. I did, however, manage to avoid trying the many deep fried insects they like to eat in the North and they do make for a ghastly display with giant bugs and maggots alongside Grasshoppers.

One option to move on from Chiang Mai is to take Thai Airways internal flight to Mae Hong Son. This amazing flight only cost 850 baht (about $22 US dollars) and flies low over the Mountains of the Hill tribe people which can be spotted from the air nestled in their small settlements. The mountains are exceptionally striking, and lakes and waterfalls can be viewed meandering through the passes. Mae Hong Son is the main province for the area and many of the hill tribe treks into the mountains start here.

The town is extremely beautiful, with a large, very ornate Wat (temple), called Wat Johnkam-Jongklang. The Wat borders a stunning lake in the centre of town and in the evening the reflection on the water shimmers with the many candles that are lit. This is the furthest North West Corner of Thailand, close to the border with Burma, so my travels now turn East again to Chiang Kong and the River Mekong.

Walking the plank to get on the slow boat going down the River Mekong to Lao

A full boat

Chapter 7 - A female Nomad in Lao

"Seek and you will find. Don't be willing to accept an ordinary life."
Salle Merrill Redfield

Journey down the River Mekong

I left Chaing Mai with another lone female backpacker, also from
England, called Linda, and we spent 6 tiresome hours on a mini-
bus to Chang Klong. We had the reprieve of a comfy bed at
Chang Klong before being rudely awakened at 6.00 a.m. by the
yapping of dogs and the constant cock-a-doodle do' of the cocks.
That day we would continue our journey to Laung Prabang, Lao,
by slow boat down the Mekong River. It sounded so romantic, a 2-
day trip through beautiful countryside down the Mekong. We were
hustled into the mini-buses before we had chance to finish our
breakfast properly, and quickly paid for the sandwiches made up
for the trip ahead. Eventually, with all the packs stacked tightly into
the van, we took the 5-minute ride to immigration to check out of
Thailand. Before we knew it, we were loaded into another van and
another 5-minute journey to the Port.

The ferry across to Lao was by 'long-tail boat', long wooden
canoes that use long propellers to drive the boat. The engine is
exposed and could be from any type of previously used machinery
that required a diesel engine, so they are never the same size and
usually result in a noisy ride. These boats are used all over Asia
by the fishermen as well as for the tourist trade and are usually
decorated with garlands of colourful ribbons and fake orchid
garlands, to bring good luck. It is unusual to see a 'long-tail'
converted for use with the quieter 'outboard motor' since this is a
much more expensive way to run the boat (and quieter isn't
necessarily better in Thailand). As we reach the shore, we loaded
the packs again, hauled them on our backs like donkeys, and
trudged up the hill for Lao's immigration and the transfer to the
port for the 'slow-boat'. Around 60 people crowded onto an old
long wooden narrow boat, completely enclosed by a low roof, not
high enough for western people, with open wooden frames for
windows.

Diary excerpt

Everyone jostles for his or her own bit of space and Linda and I sit straight backed on a little wooden bench with a plank of wood as back-support. We look at each other and pick our way through the legs, feet and packs to check out the seating arrangement at the back of the boat. Mats on the floor somehow seem more attractive, even though we do notice that we've passed the open diesel engine on the way. We spot a crude bunk, which must belong to one of the crew, and decide to be a bit cheeky and climb up into it. What have we got to lose? Our legs are fitted together somehow and we both recline back with our books, giggling. I look down at all the other passengers crowded together on the mats and ask 'how come none of you thought of this?'

We had 30 minutes of pleasure until the engine fired up and we realized we'd picked the worst place on the boat. The noise was deafening from the open diesel and the room soon filled up with thick blue smoke. As we made a quick exit, hoping there were some seats left further forward, Linda commented on the dead rats floating in the bilge water. The rest of the passengers probably laughed at our situation, now the last people to find seats! We struggled forward remembering to dip our heads at every cross-beam, but despite the caution, still nearly knocked ourselves out on more than one occasion. The front of the boat was more airy and away from the engine, so quieter. We all looked like cattle squeezed together on our little wooden benches, feeling the vibrations of the boat and wilting in the heat. Welcome to the Mekong River. Maybe it used to be peaceful, but not anymore.

These big wooden noisy boats ply up and down the river, dodging the fast boats that zoom along at 40 mph swerving around rocks and shallows. The fast boats are so noisy they give their passengers crash helmets to quieten the noise a little, but also to give them a fighting chance should the boat slam into a rock at that speed. We have 6 hours in total on this boat before a nights rest and back on again for another 6 hours of torture the next day.

We spend the time chatting to the other passengers on the boat and we meet some other lone travellers who are heading for the same place. Lee is from Canada and she has met up with Jenny who is also from Canada, Julia is from Australia and her travelling companion is Mani (a guy) who is travelling from South Africa. Although we didn't plan it at the time, we all end up travelling together and celebrating Christmas and the New Year in each others' company.

The following day starts early again from Pakbang, where we stopped in a guesthouse with bamboo walls so thin, you could even hear the whispers of the room next to you. Last night Tom (one of the other lone backpackers who has 'joined' our group) read some graffiti on the walls of his room, warning other guests to remove food from the room, otherwise face the consequences of rats visiting in the night. You could hear the rustle of plastic bags as everyone retreated to the outside balcony with their bags of supplies, to hang them on a ceiling nail.

By 6.30 am everyone is up and drinking Lao coffee mixed with thick sweet condensed milk. Some were brave enough to take turns with the cold shower on the chilly morning, whilst others departed early in the hope of getting the 'best seats' on the boat. Some had opted to change for the 'fast boat' and run the risk of the rapids and the danger. We'd been told 8 hours until we reach Laung Prabang, but yesterday was suppose to be 6 hours and turned out to be 7, so let's hope another hour isn't added to the day's journey. The morning is cold and everyone is wrapped up in as many clothes as they possess or had the forethought to take out of their backpacks.

Diary excerpt

We had a delay this morning whilst they loaded planks of wood onto the boat, slowly stealing more and more leg room from the passengers. Later, we discovered they had not stacked the wood evenly, so the boat heeled dangerously to one side every time we negotiated a rapid. The more seasoned travellers are dressed warmly, sporting earplugs or CD players to drown the sound of the loud diesel engine. The less seasoned ones look cold and miserable.

The scenery is magnificent but difficult to observe with the low windows. Every now and then we spot a tiny settlement by the river with no obvious road access through the mountains, all their supplies arrive by boat. We stop at a couple of the bigger

113

settlements and the passengers disembark to buy cold drinks served in plastic bags. You soon get used to this Asian way of serving cold drinks, first they put ice, if available, in the bag, and then pour the juice over the ice, pop in a straw, and secure the top of the bag with elastic, a bit like they do at the fair-grounds when they give a gold-fish away! You can never be too sure what you are drinking, the usual sodas are sometimes available, but more often than not you will be drinking coconut milk, tang mix or ice coffee or something brightly coloured which could be anything. All the passengers scan the make-shift market stalls for edible food (or food they recognise) and the crew off-load supplies for the village from the top of the boat.

The journey in total took 16 hours broken by the night spent in Pakbang. We heard lots of stories from other travellers about their boat experiences, and it seems we must have picked a particularly busy day and a particularly bad boat. Some travellers had the luxury of sitting on low windows with their legs dangling in the Mekong, others lounged with plenty of space, and so it sounds like we had bad luck. I still think the journey was worth it though to be able to see Laung Prabang.

Laung Prabang – City of Temples

Laung Prabang has one road which runs through the centre of the city, lined with restaurants and shops, the rest is more a small town with dusty pot-holed lanes, scattered with stones and surrounded by coconut palms and banana trees. Hiring a bicycle is a wonderful way to enjoy the atmosphere of the old city, and so a few of the group hired one for the day, observing young monks walking along in their orange robes and matching umbrellas. The school children share bicycles, the passenger on the back, balancing an umbrella for shade and holding their long silk skirts, which they wear as part of their uniform.

Diary excerpt

Within 5 minutes we felt like we had left the city and rode on rough stone-strewn roads with breathtaking views of the lush green mountains. Nestled high on the hill was Paan Pao temple, an unusual Buddhist temple with murals on the walls depicting the atrocities carried out by humans, against humans, before Buddha brought love, peace and respect. The Buddhist temple on the hill

114

*commands incredible views over Nam Khan River on one side
and the Mekong on the other. In the distance of the Nam Khan
you can see the sparkling stupa of Vat Paan Poo we visited
yesterday, nestled amongst the mountains. As the sun set across
the valley, the novice monks sound the large drums and cymbals
adding to the atmosphere as we descended the 322 steps back to
street level.*

The incredible thing about Laung Prabang is the surrounding
countryside and the insight into Lao culture within a 10-minute
drive. Hiring a motorbike would be a wonderful way to see the
sights, but in reality, the roads are so poor, and many travellers
bear the scars of the falls you must expect to take. You are
responsible for your own safety and in some places the road has
slipped down the mountain calling for some careful navigation.

Our group of seven hired a songtheaw (a small open cabin with 2
rows of benches facing each other), and an experienced driver, to
take us the 35 kms ride through the outstanding countryside, to a
waterfall we'd read about in our travel guides. Within 10 minutes
the road had turned into a dirt track and we were passing water
buffalos walking in an orderly line, farmers carrying baskets
balanced on poles across their shoulders, and children playing.

The mountains are incredibly enchanting and as we climbed
higher, we crossed small bridges across the river, indicating the
waterfall was getting closer. None of us had expectations for the
visual smorgasbord we were about to witness. How do you
describe a place so beautiful? We literally stopped in our tracks
and our jaws dropped in unison at the incredible height of the
tiered waterfall cascading through the rich rainforest. The water
was crystal clear tumbling into turquoise pools before overflowing
to the next pool as far as the eyes could see. We climbed to a
vantage point until we could feel the water in the air and sat
staring at the magnificent beauty of the water. Looking down into
the valley the sparking green pools shimmered in the light. We
clambered down, picking our way across mini-falls, sometimes
above our knees in the little pools, sometimes navigating slippery
rocks or balancing across fallen logs. The overwhelming beauty of
the pools was too inviting to resist, despite the low sun and cold
water.

Diary excerpt

We hung our clothes on a nearby tree and plunged into the first sparkling pool. We swam against the flow, close to the first mini-fall, where the water bubbled and sparkled like a Jacuzzi bath. Surrounded by giant vegetation and bamboo the spectacle was quite overwhelming. Tom swam to the next overfall and peered over the edge to the larger deeper pool, and suddenly jumped off the edge with a whelp of delight. We all quickly followed, only Linda and I hesitating at the edge before taking the plunge. How exhilarating! We clambered over larger rocks to the next pool that was set in an oasis of smaller falls on each side. In this pool you could swim towards one of the outer falls which would then carry you back by the flow. If the sun had not been so low I would have loved to continue our investigation of the lower pools until they eventually seized to exist, but our bodies were beginning to shiver which told us it was time to exit.

Our songtheaw awaited us to start the one-hour journey back. As the sun set we watched the ever-changing colours of the sky as the bright red sky reflected off the mountains. As suddenly as the sun disappeared behind a mountain, the full moon rose spectacularly. We all took group photos of the giant white globe low in the sky and just stared at the incredible scene it painted. As the light faded, the pot-holed road ahead became a theatre of frogs leaping across the headlights.

Journey to Vang Viang - 21st December 2002

Diary excerpt

As the mini van climbs up to the clear blue skies, the valley below is blanketed in soft white clouds. The tops of the mountains are bathed in morning light reflecting on the blankets below. Small settlements of bamboo huts are nestled on the hillsides and we pass children laughing and waving on the roadside. The mini bus dodges chickens, goats, pigs and puppies as it negotiates the sharp curves and potholes. The road snakes around the low cloud basin below, the intensity of the white glow strengthens. A herd of goats is around the next bend, a very pregnant mother and a cackle of kids, they do not appear to be supervised by people.

Children walk along the side of the road, carrying bushels of grass which we saw drying in the previous village to repair roofs. The van slows for a section of the road that has mostly fallen away into the deep valley below. Small bamboo huts cling onto the sides of the hill with apparently no road or path to them. The people in these villages have not been touched by western 'advancement'. They live a simple self-sufficient life-style, farming the land and raising cattle and chickens. They are always smiling and singing, they don't realize how beautiful the land they live in is, they probably yearn for western luxuries like electricity or water on tap, whilst the luxury mini bus full of white people secretly yearn for their simple life. The mist lifts from the valley revealing the sparkling river below. Despite the cramped uncomfortable conditions in the mini-van, I never want this particular road journey to end.

One of the advantages of travelling in a group is that we were able to hire the mini-van together to take us to our next destination. Often as a lone traveller it is more difficult to find transport in these less travelled places and you have to find other travellers who want to go to the same destination before you can hire someone. In this respect, our group of 7 gave us all the benefits of booking 'bulk' transport, although at times, we all wished to be alone and not part of the dynamics of a large group. The number seven was not that convenient when it came to sharing accommodation and someone always had to pay the price of a single room, which often caused dissent. The fact there was 2 males in the group was quite insignificant, it didn't really matter who you shared with, although as time moved on 'favourites' graduated together. I was a good 10 years older than everyone else in the group so I tended to take a back step when the dynamics of a big group started to cause problems.

Monks at Vat Thamphosi

Our Christmas bungalow on the river at Vang Viang

Hiring a bicycle and navigating the cobble streets of
Luang Prabang

My original travelling partner, Linda, started to behave more like a 2 week tourist than a traveller, complaining about the road trip, and lack of rest stops with no facilities and favouring some of the younger members of the group who had mp3 players and the latest music. It amazed me that some completely missed the scenery, sleeping most of the way through, and that a couple of the other girls preferred to read their travel guides to learn about their next road trip they would miss.

The limestone Karst Mountains of Vang Viang - 22nd December 2002

Diary excerpt

I don't know what time it is this evening, time has no significance here, but the moon is just rising and only 2 days after full, so I would estimate 8.00 pm. I'm walking back alone to my riverside cottage; everyone I pass on the street respectively nods and greets me 'sabadee'. I stumble a little on the stones in the dark and a group of travellers of European nationality stop to show me the way with their flash lights. I greet an Italian lady and her daughter as I pass her through the gates to my guesthouse. She

119

greets me hello and her daughter smiles and says hi. It is completely impossible not to smile or greet strangers here if you're travelling alone.

This feels like the kind of place you would want to live out the rest of your years. It is so incredibly beautiful it defies the correct words to describe it. A unique blend of traditional Lao life with all the comforts of the western world, no wonder everyone is smiling.

I ate a meal tonight equivalent to a 5 star restaurant. A beautiful outside setting with good music at exactly the right volume, candles on the table, and a festive spirit with Christmas lights providing the only other light. Pepper steak cooked in cream and brandy with a fresh green salad and a delicious dressing, washed down with (several) glasses of welcome red wine. The waitresses are dressed in traditional Lao skirts with those amazing smiling faces, eager to please. So attentive they anticipate your needs before you feel the need to beckon them for assistance. All this is available at prices that make you smile, $2 for dinner, $6 for a comfortable room, a good glass of wine less than a dollar. Our riverside bungalow has 3 beds so I am sharing with Tom and Linda, it was the only accommodation left being so close to Christmas and although $18 seems pretty pricey for our own bungalow we decided it was worth the treat. We have a large picture window which looks out directly onto the river and our own sunbathing balcony where we can watch the other travellers play on the river on their rubber tubes.

The other travellers in our group opted to share rooms in a cheaper hostel close to the town, but we ended up bumping into each other anyway since the town is so small. As soon as cheaper accommodation was available we moved into another shared room with 3 beds, but enjoyed the luxury of the riverside bungalow whilst we were there (we were told later that Kylie Minouge actually slept in that same bungalow with a boyfriend when she visited a few years ago).

Diary excerpt

As I walked home I glanced upwards to the evening sky and stopped in my tracks gazing at the incredible phenomenon of sparkling stars sitting on a gentle bed of soft white clouds aglow with the light of the rising moon. I smiled at the memory of the *giant rubber tube I hired for $1.50. I floated down the river with a group of friends, consuming the beauty of the mountains and relaxing in the sunshine. What a day!*

The giant limestone Karst Mountains provide the perfect backdrop to the clean sparkling Nam Xong River, with tiny islands turned into 'Beer Lao' riverside bars and enough rapids to keep you on your toes after a drink or two. The smiling Lao women try to catch you with long bamboo poles as you speed past in your inner tube, and navigate your tube to ensure you don't miss their particular riverside bar. Several of the stop points have signs pointing you to the caves, some of which you can take your tube into to explore the waterways inside. We had such a giggle, the seven of us all forming a large circle as we drifted down the river together and holding onto each others inner tubes, passing beers and cigarettes between us.

We all complained of cold bums (they dangled in the cold water) and we fooled around trying to balance on our tubes holding them out of the water, some of us tipping up and ending up completely soaked. We spotted a Beer Lao bar on a sunny bank and all decided to head for it forming a line holding onto each other as we tried to steer our way towards the Lao ladies with the long bamboo poles. Once one of us had grabbed a pole we helped each other climb onto the sunny bank and dry out our wet pants! Sharing the last of our soggy cigarettes and enjoying a cold beer we planned our return to the water, spotting a fast area ahead with some dangerous looking boulders that would require some careful navigation.

As soon as you let the giant inner tube float you took off quickly in the fast current and most of us lost our grip of trying to hold onto each other as we tumbled in the current. I recovered in time to notice I was heading straight for a large boulder sticking out of the water. I quickly decided I was on a collision course with the rock and that the best course of action would be to 'land' on it, rather than collide with it, which I successfully did. Much to the amusement of everyone else around I was suddenly stranded, high and dry, on a pinnacle boulder surrounded by fast flowing water, with no way off! The group knew about my back problems and Jennifer immediately rushed to my rescue, abandoning her inner tube to rescue me by fighting against the current to come to

121

my aid! Once more, another example of the virtues of travelling in a group!

We quickly tired of water activities, and hired a bike for a dollar the following day, crossing the river to explore the paddy fields and 2 large caves we had heard about. We followed rough hand written signs into the jungle and was greeted by a Lao girl under a grass hut waiting for visitors. She took a nominal fee from us and provided basic head lamps which we giggled at. The large head lamps were heavy on our heads and the battery packs were really cumbersome, like little mini car batteries with open wires connecting to your head lamp. It meant you could only walk with one hand and you had to keep un-tangling the wires to your head from the pack so you didn't get them caught on anything! We were then left at the top of the rickety steps at the entrance to the dark cave, to explore alone, and told to watch out for the spiders and the large deep crevices! Needless to say, we didn't stay long, our first sighting of the giant spiders was enough to make us turn back!

I've read critical articles about Vang Viang and I cannot even begin to comprehend how anybody could even think any negative thoughts about this incredibly wonderful place. Lao reminds me a little of Madagascar, which is probably my next favourite place in the world. I've visited over 37 countries and Lao simply sits on the top of that pile very comfortably. Everyone searches for something when they're travelling, but deep down, you want to experience the true culture of the countries you visit without the discomfort of having to actually 'live' their culture. We can all 'rough it' for a few days to live with the 'hill tribe' people, eat their food, sleep on hard bamboo floors and shiver in the cool night air. I wouldn't disparage these experiences, I lived plenty of them as I've travelled around and my heart has been warmed by the chance to experience that way of living. But the opportunity to experience life both ways? Of course we all smile. This morning I woke early and walked to the morning market and smiled at the Lao culture surviving strong and hard in this place which now caters for the western tourist, and somehow, it all fits perfectly. I hope it stays that way forever; there is a good chance it will.

Dok Kihounkham Island – Nam Ngum Lake - 27th December 2002

The last few days in Vang Viang were overcast and dull with rain. It completely changes the appearance of the town, turning pretty sand roads into muddy puddles and shrouding the mountains in low cloud. Low tractor vehicles tow rough wooden trailers piled high with Lao girls clasping umbrellas. The overcast conditions and overflowing drains, somehow allows you to leave, and so today the whole group heads for the Lake.

Travelling on a songtheaw through the mountain villages is always a delightful way to observe village life. Days are filled with repairing their bamboo huts, tending the many chicken, pigs and cattle and looking after the many children. Our first sight of the lake from a vantage point on the road revealed green water dotted with islands and a backdrop of mountains shrouded in cloud. We were taken down to the boat dock for the short ride across the lake to Dok Khounkham Island.

The island looks like a jungle and we cannot see any likely accommodation, but as we pull into a small bay a brick guesthouse is revealed. We clamber out of the boats and are shown to our respective rooms. Dirty cream painted walls, an old wooden floor and a hard bed with a thin blanket. The bathroom is a broken western toilet and a badly cracked sink and a cold-water tap and bucket for your shower. We all pray that the sun will rise tomorrow to brighten our spirits and provide nice weather to explore the island and the lake. The dynamics of the large group comes into play once again, Linda suddenly decides to share a room with someone other than me or Tom without telling us and the rest of the group rush to the largest room with the best view and a balcony, and start arguing about who is going to stay in that room. I end up sharing with Tom, which I didn't mind, but we didn't have very much in common and the small shared bathroom was difficult to negotiate when you are trying to maintain your privacy.

Kayaking down the River

The sun obliged and we woke to it teasing the shimmering green water. A lazy day of lounging in the hammocks and reading books was completed by a boat trip around the islands to watch the sunset. Whilst planning our departure to Vientiane we were asked if we would like to kayak there. What a fantastic way to travel with ours bags arranged to meet us there. The group grew to 9 and we departed from the lake to start our journey down the River Ngum. Our first obstacle as we launched ourselves into the river was to quickly paddle across stream to take advantage of the rapids. Shrieking with delight some took a tumble and others delighted in watching their antics. The river quickly quietened to a slow flow and our Lao guide gently began to sing traditional songs as we silently paddled, consuming the incredible beauty surrounding us.

Diary excerpt

As we glided across the green water we passed small farming communities, tending their vegetables in neat rows lining the banks of the river. Groups of small naked children dashed from their bamboo huts as they spotted the colourful possession making its way down the river, and screeched with delight, waving and shouting 'sabadee'. This Lao greeting translated as 'hello' but had a lovely sing song quality about it. A little further down stream it was bathing time and a group of children were jumping off a high bank and splashing into the river, whilst the women bathed in sarongs or did their laundry. Small wooden boats occasionally passed us paddling upstream, loaded with vegetables with colourful Lao women dressed in traditional straw hats greeting us 'sabadee' as they passed.

The sun beat down and we were all beginning to suffer from over exposure and tried to aim our kayaks into shady areas. Our legs were exposed directly in the sun, most of us opting to wear shorts knowing we would get wet, but Julia and Jenny were both fair skinned and we all watched as their legs turned pink and then red in the sun. Nobody knew the journey was going to take so long and most were exhausted by the long trip and badly sunburnt. Lucky for me I was wearing trousers and I had the Lao guide to take over my paddling when I tired, opting for a shared kayak rather than my own, like most selected. Linda was particularly angry at the length of the journey and seemed to want to take it out on me. The journey ended at a Riverside restaurant where a traditional Lao meal greeted us and prepared us for the further one-hour songtheaw journey to Vientiane.

124

Vientiane - French Cosmopolitan meets the Lao Tradition

A curious mix of French cosmopolitan and traditional Lao, a city with a heavy French influence, thronging with western tourist dining in 5 star restaurants with high quality European food at inflated Lao prices. The atmosphere could trick you into forgetting you are still in Lao, until you discover there is no international ATM machine, no Western Union, unreliable slow internet service, and city streets which turn into villages at the drop of a hat. Dine in a fine restaurant with well trained staff and amazing food and then step out into the street facing a pile of garbage randomly piled, and drains, some covered with uneven stones, others completely open and awaiting the next victim.

Although we all arrived as a group and booked into the same hostel, this marked the end of our travels together and I witnessed little groups splitting off and deciding where to go next. I was sharing a room with Linda again but she was expecting to meet up with another friend from England who she would stay with. This immediately caused problems because she didn't want to commit to sharing with me after her friend arrived. Some room shuffling with other members of the group eventually meant I was sharing with Linda and her friend in a room with 3 beds.

Through Linda's friend, I met CJ, and we hit it off immediately, struggling to find any common ground with the two girls who spent a good hour styling their hair and doing their make-up before going out to eat. CJ is an English teacher living on the river Mekong and she quickly invited me to stay with her once she realised everyone else was moving on and I would have to pay triple for the room I had now committed to.

I was very fortunate to have been invited to spend a few days staying by the Mekong in a traditional Lao wooden house in a small 'village' community. I ended up staying with CJ for 5 days and quickly settled into her humble home, sleeping on the wooden floor on a thin mattress and visiting the market each day to buy fresh vegetables to make dinner for her when she returned from school.

It was like being on the boat again, truly integrating into the culture of the country, shopping with the locals and fetching water for the neighbours. It was here in CJ's house I started to work on the idea of a book and I spent most days writing on her computer and copying to disk.

The 97-year-old lady who shared the garden, outside cooking area and communal sweeping brush, smiled when I helped her clean the cooking area outside and she mumbled constantly in Lao grinning and showing her red mouth rotted with years of chewing bettle. CJ who has been living here for 3 years speaks fluent Lao and understands and joked with her all the time.

Diary excerpt:

The community is close and welcoming and CJ tells me tales of the times everyone has helped her when she was bed-ridden by a motorcycle accident and when she had her appendix out. She explained to me some of the interesting facts I didn't know about the country, such as the origin of the name. It has been called Lao PDR since 1975 when it became independent from French colonial rule, when, prior, the country was called Laos. These days the rest of the world still calls Lao PDR, Laos, which is politically wrong. Lao PDR rarely refers to itself as Laos. .People and the language are called 'Lao people' and the 'Lao language' respectively. It is O.K. to shorten the name to Lao but whenever you do this, outside the country, you'll find people try to correct you by saying 'oh you mean Laos', with a heavy emphasis on the 's'. sound.

Tonight she has been invited to a wedding party and as they waited for her, the old lady was giggling and pointing at her outfit advising what she should wear with her traditional Lao skirt. Eventually, CJ shrugged her shoulders and the old lady rushed next door and returned with a peasants blouse and insisted she put it on. CJ obeyed but refused to change her motorbike boots or leather jacket that she always wears when riding her motorcycle.

I continue to pack by candlelight ready for my flight tomorrow to Cambodia; it will be a sad day that I leave this beautiful country and its warm, genuine and friendly people.

Chapter 8 - Cambodia and the ancient ruins of Angkor Wat

"If you want others to be happy, practice compassion; if you want to be happy, practice compassion"
Dalai lama

I arrived here alone after taking the plane from Vientiane to the Capital Phnom Penn and then stopping overnight in Phnom Penn to break up the journey to Siem Reap. I was looking for someone to share a taxi with and spotted a backpacker just getting into a taxi as I came out of the airport doors. There was no one else around and I had already been warned about taking taxi's alone, putting yourself at risk of being charged silly prices or being dropped off at *their* choice of hotel. I started to run after the taxi waving my arms and shouting for it to stop, grabbing the back door handle just as it was about to accelerate away. This is where I met Katherine, another English girl travelling alone and also a little nervous of the taxi ride, and agreed to share the ride with me.

I asked her where she was staying and the taxi driver immediately answered saying he knew where to take us (I bet he did). It took some convincing to get him to drop us near to a hostel I had already selected from my guide book, and located on the river. He had obviously decided where Katherine was going to stay and he was not happy about me changing his plans! He got his revenge on me by stopping the taxi about a mile from our destination saying that he would not drive on the rough road which took him down to the river and our chosen accommodation. We had no choice and had to bale out where he told us to, stranded on a rough road in the middle of nowhere with our backpacks at our feet!

At this point I think Katherine regretted allowing me to get in her taxi and select our accommodation and looked at me for inspiration of where we should go next! At that moment a friendly motor bike stopped at our feet and smiled at our situation, one he had obviously come across a few times, and offered to give us a lift to our accommodation on the river. It turned out the taxi's did not like to take people to these rooms because the city hotels paid them commission to take people there straight from the airport but they did not get paid commission to take guests to our chosen accommodation. The motorbike boy gestured to join him on his seat and Katherine looked at me questioning if we could both fit on with our back packs! Silly question really, it is not unusual to see whole families and the dog loaded onto these mopeds in the same way the Western world uses a family car! The experience was quite entertaining, 2 girls with large backpacks wobbling down the street on a small moped, laughing and giggling all the way!

He took us directly to our accommodation, which turned out to be a lovely location right on the river, and happily headed back up the road to meet the next victims! I spent a lovely evening chatting with Katherine and we planned to take the boat together the next day to Siem Reap and maybe visit some of the sites together once we got there. It was always much more fun travelling with someone and it always worked out much cheaper to share a room rather than take a room by yourself. I was still living on the money we had taken out of our joint bank account in Malaysia and it wouldn't stretch too much further if I didn't stick to the $10 a day rule.

The following day we boarded the express boat from Phnom Penn to Siem Reap, a 5 hour journey down the River which I'd planned to take 2 days, but now took less than a day. I don't think these boats had been offering this service for long, but they were old with no amenities, They had a very strange toilet which I couldn't figure out how to use, it was an Asian standing toilet but it was raised so high you could not climb up to use it. Just imagine the sight when you open the door to find a raised porcelain bowl with 2 foot imprints (this is where you are suppose to put your feet when you 'hover' over the ground version) but at waist height! It is as though they designed a western toilet (one which would take a seat) but still installed the standard porcelain bowl. Well it meant neither the western or the Asian people could actually use it, which was one way of keeping it clean but very inconvenient for a 5 hour boat ride! It did provide some quite interesting entertainment though as you watched the unsuspecting victim opening the door and scratching their heads at the sight!

Diary excerpt:

The River Basccac and Tonle Sap Lake seem to be the life-line for the people here. The difference between here and Lao is the countryside, and this seems to add a certain sadness. The soil is rough and clay-like, the vegetable plots on the banks of the river

*haphazard and struggling to survive, there doesn't seem to be any
mature vegetation and even the palm trees don't look healthy.
Still the children wave and smile at the big fast express boat that
goes by with the white tourist. The people here work the river, live
in stilted bamboo houses balancing on the banks and skull their
rough wooden canoes across the wide river. The poverty is
everywhere, and then a pile of modern red bricks and a flash of
orange robes - money being poured into another new temple. The
floating houses (and whole villages of them) look inhospitable.*

*The only flashes of colour are the hats or scarves of the
fishermen. Everywhere is so flat and parched and desolate and
brown, such a contrast to Lao. A beautiful bird skims across the
water, it looks a little like a kingfisher but is white and grey, large
white geese flicker in the sunlight. A mountain is in the distance;
although it has some vegetation it doesn't have the same lush
green colour of Lao. Still the people smile and the children wave
eagerly, maybe the tourist has come to save them. Another
enjoyable boat ride which gave me an invaluable insight into the
culture of the river people of Cambodia.*

SIEM REAP is another story, less than 10 years ago it was
relatively unfrequented as a tourist destination. Now it is a
premier historical site in S.E. Asia and its rich cultural history is
widely accessible. Many people think that Angkor Wat is the only
monument, but Angkor actually covers an area of over 77 square
miles in North West Cambodia, with over 40 accessible sites. The
name Angkor means 'holy city' and has a rich history dating back
to the 10th Century. The generally accepted dates for the Angkor
period are 802 to 1432 and are designated as the period which
the Khmer empire reached its greatest territorial limits and its
apogee in cultural and artistic achievements.

The founder of Angkor was King Jayavarman II who established a
new religious belief, the devaraja god-king cult. Successive kings
after Jayavarman II continued to unify and expand the Khmer
Empire. The inscriptions give the names of 39 kings from the
Angkor period. Indravarthan set a precedent for future kings by
building a temple mountain which became a means for successive
rulers to display their omnipotence. The last major king was
Jayavarman VII (1181-1220) and undertook a massive building
program and is accredited for constructing more monuments,
roads and bridges than all the other kings put together.

Subsequent battles with Indonesia and Thailand eventually saw the capital move because of Angkor's proximity to the enemy. The kingdom shifted south east to Phnom Penh in the 15th century as a more suitable base to develop interests in the maritime trade in S.E.Asia.

Although the ruins of Angkor were reported as early as the 16th century it wasn't until 1855 that the western world took an interest following a lively and interesting article written by Dr A House, an American missionary. Subsequent French expeditions in 1866 led by Ernest Doudart de Laquee systematically publicized Angkor to the outside world and led to EFEO to study and disengage the historical sites from the jungle. Today, many of the site ruins are still tangled in the jungle roots and this is what makes these sites unique to visit. It seems incredible to imagine that this now barren land was once the land of kings with splendour and riches beyond anything in Western history.

In an historical declaration during a visit to Angkor Wat in November 1991, Federal Major, Director General of UNESCO declared 'Angkor, City of the Khmer Kings" and this led to international participation in saving Angkor. In 1992 it was included on the UNESCO World Heritage list of over 400 sites recognizing Angkor as one of mankind's most significant cultural heritage sites and the International symbol of Cambodia and its people. By 1993 the new Royal Government of Cambodia assumed the responsibility of protecting and maintaining historic monuments realizing their potential as tourist attractions. I reminded myself that less than 10 years ago I would not have been able to visit this country and that independent travellers would not have been able to see these amazing historical heritage sites. This must have been the best time to visit, before tourism began to destroy the unique culture of Cambodia.

Siam Reap has responded to this with good tree lined roads to the temples and a wide variety of restaurants, hotels and guest houses. The infrastructure is still developing so I saw tourists with large hard suitcases struggling off the express boat into a deluge of locals holding welcome signs on a rough muddy bank in the middle of a mangrove island (the nearest river port to Siam Reap). At the time of writing, you could stay in a $300 dollar room but you still had to arrive the same way as the backpacker, who could probably find accommodation for a few dollars!

You can now fly Thai airways direct from Bangkok, and in January 2007 the first direct flights to Phonm Penn started from Vancouver, B.C. Canada. However, judging by the number of digital camera's and video's monitoring the display on the mangrove island, this way of travelling obviously adds to the whole cultural experience and gave the higher class tourists the rare opportunity to glimpse the real Cambodia. They probably pay a premium now to take the express boat rather than the direct flight!

Angkor Wat has introduced many more employment opportunities, but the greatest desire of many of the young boys I met was to be a tour guide. They know the standards are high so they practice their English and try and learn and memorise the history of the temples. The backpacker provides the learning platform, charging the same price it would cost to hire a motorcycle yourself, they rent themselves to drive you (as pillion passenger on their own motorcycle) so that they can practise their knowledge. It is a great way for the traveller to get an insight into the culture of these boys, and I found it just as interesting talking to them, as hearing about the ancient temples.

My guide was called Nat and he was 20 years old, he worked from my guesthouse and had been using the money he gets as a motorbike guide to attend the night school four and half hours a week to study English literature. He hopes this education will allow him to be a writer, a teacher, or a tour guide. When he lived at home on his family's farm, his job was to look after 10 cows and his 3 brothers and 3 sisters, but as they grew older and more independent, the farm was not big enough to provide for everyone, so he chose to leave home to become a novice monk for 10 years so that he could learn basic English skills, so that he could then move to Siem Reap.

As an unofficial guide he earns around $200 a month and his school fees are $390 a year, leaving enough to help support his family. He was hoping to get work as a government teacher or as an 'official' tour guide which pays around $7,000 US a year (the tour guides are regulated by the tour company's and they have to pay for their own insurance). However, Nat says, as long as his English is good he will have lots of options open to him, even if he has to work in a restaurant which gives him free accommodation

131

(but not food…). It sometimes makes we wonder if we had to work so hard to pay for our education if we would appreciate it more! Even very young children aspire to the same goal as Nat, and hoards of young children hang around at the tourist bus stops to sell pineapple or bread for the opportunity to talk English with the tourist. As soon as the bus pulls up to the stop young girls crowd you and ask "where are you from?" "How old are you?" "What is your name?" Then they eagerly tell you about their school and the name of their teachers and ask politely if you have any pens or paper to spare?

The less fortunate family resort to begging, and a crowd of land mine victims can usually be found at the bus stations and stops, competing with the young girls who want to learn English. One family I watched from the bus had made home on a rough piece of land near the bus stop. A mother and her young child lay in a hammock strung across two bare trees whilst the husband slept on a mat under a mosquito net with 3 more little bundles close to him on a sack on the floor. The younger children are not old enough to beg and the husband still has all his limbs, but can not leave his family to learn English so that he can enter the tourist trade, so his only hope was that the passing bus passengers would take pity on him and give him some change.

It is families like these that can fall victim to some of the more unsavoury characters of Cambodia who are offering 'tours' to the local orphanages to raise money in donations for the children kept in very poor conditions. In reality, many of these children are not orphans, but have been bought for as little as $20 from their poverty struck parents (in the hope that they will have a better life in the orphanage). Once in the orphanage, some of the children are then sold into the sex slavery market or exposed to paedophiles. The more tourists that visit the orphanages and donate large sums of money, the worst they are making the situation, so new awareness charities (such as licadho.org) are trying to educate the tourist who want to donate to orphanages.

The tourist trade has improved employment opportunities, with restoration workers on the temples, refuse collectors, gardeners and security jobs now available to the 'non- English speakers'. But unfortunately, the poor still end up being victims of the big developers who continually illegally grab prime land for more tourist hotels and facilities. Many of the traditional musicians and artists that survived the Khmer rouge are now being moved on to rural areas with no amenities, to make room for new development. Indeed, it is common place to hear about the "government" sweeping up the beggars like refuse, so the "tourist" does not have to deal with them, or look at their poor deformed bodies ravaged by land-mines.

The most popular form of transport is the bicycle, and it is not uncommon to see 5 or 6 bicycles abreast across the road at rush hour! The farmers can now sell their produce outside the temples at the higher price to the tourist and children learn young to produce local crafts to sell too. The Cambodians have become some of the best entrepreneurs, with young children learning English quickly, together with cheekiness and some of the best sales skills I have ever experienced! They all compete, but they also all share and are humouredly competitive. Indeed when faced with 10 young girls all trying to sell their hand-made scarf to you, it is difficult to choose which ones you should buy from (I ended up with 10 scarves). They are never aggressive or rude; they always smile and are very polite. The lucky ones wear flip-flops whilst most are bare-foot wearing dirty tatty clothes and unkept hair.

I spent a week in Cambodia visiting the temples with Katherine, who then left me to visit the 'killing fields'. I didn't fancy seeing the famous pile of human skulls, so decided to return to Thailand, following an email from my niece who was shortly arriving for a holiday.

This resourceful nation of people is never defeated by something as simple as an unreliable old bus, and on the bus trip I took to return to Thailand, we were held up for several hours whilst our bus was pushed across a rickety bridge. Each time the bus changed gears you could hear the screeching, especially shifting down gear, and finally the bus stalled on the bridge, blocking both ways of ever-increasing traffic, to anything other than a bicycle.

Diary excerpt:

Everyone joins in to push the bus across the bridge and to one side of the road so that the men can scratch their heads together and work out what emergency repairs can be carried out. It only took 25 minutes and plenty of people helping, to repair the gear box but in the meantime I noted some of the vehicles which passed us. A motorcycle has 4 passengers, the father driving with his wife behind clutching her young daughter and her young son balanced on the rack over the back wheel. A truck is loaded with more than 20 workers, probably farmers because they are wearing many layers of clothes and hats and scarves to protect them from the sun (which is very hot for them but they seem to prefer this to the damaging/darkening effects of the sun). Two bikes riding side by side share the load of a giant ice block balanced between them, they leave a trail of water behind them as the ice melts in the sun. Another 2 motorbikes have 2 live pigs tied as pillion passengers, lying on their backs, with trotters in the air. One motorbike was pilled high with coconuts, another with a stack of logs. Just the local Cambodians getting on with everyday life using whatever transport is available to ship their goods from one village to the next without the luxury of refrigerated trucks for ice or meat or the family car.

The road is dusty and rough, with lots of potholes and very uneven, it is not surprising they can not keep their clothes clean! This reminds me of a joke that Nat had told me:
"A man goes to a party wearing his old clothes, everyone else is in new clothes, and so no one will talk to him or give him food or drink. He decides to go home and comes back wearing new clothes. Now everyone talks to him and they ask him why he is putting the food up the sleeves of his jacket. He replies, you are not talking to me, but my clothes, so I feed my clothes, not me."
He found this joke very funny, so I laughed along (a little sadly). His next joke was even better. "A cow and a pig cross the river which is infested with crocodiles. The pig swims across the river and is not eaten, the cow does not make it. Why? Because the crocodiles are Muslim" (good job I knew that Muslims can't eat pork otherwise I wouldn't have got that one...)

The next time the bus stops it is because the road ahead is blocked again, because the bridge ahead has collapsed so we may have to wait a few hours whilst the resourceful Cambodians, re-build the bridge. I use the opportunity to find a toilet and nip off into the dry barren landscape in search of somewhere to squat. Keeping an eye open for unexploded bombs, I find a clearing marked by human waste and a few wet patches and some discarded toilet paper, it is not entirely out of the view of the bus, but I do not dare to go further off the path, so I make do. I am now

*beginning to look a little more like the locals with muddy feet and
dirty hands. As I join the waiting passengers, the Cambodians
delight in joking with the tourist and ask me if I have brought my
mat with me? "You will have to sleep the night here if the bridge
isn't mended." Of course they may not have been joking, but
fortunate for me the bridge was eventually mended and we set off
on our journey once again. I'm sure that if I had to stay the night,
someone would have shared their mat with me.*

Koh Samui and the land of consumerism

So I had now completed my rough circle and was back in Bangkok
to decide what I should do with my future. My niece was visiting
from England and staying on Koh Samui, which I had not visited,
so I decided I should head back down there to meet up with her.
Koh Samui has attracted the masses through marketing and
undoubtedly its cultural ecology has suffered. The multi-nationals
have moved in, McDonalds, Burger King, Pizza Hut and even
Starbucks, have all recognised the consumer potential of this
tourist haven and wasted no time in exploiting it. Money is a
powerful demon and the bottom line is that Thai culture cannot
absorb the effects of western consumerism without losing
something of its own uniqueness.

It was the beginning of the end of my love for Thailand and its
people and the start of a series of events which led me to leave
South East Asia altogether. All the things I had learnt about
Thailand, all the things I loved about Thailand, were suddenly
compromised. It was as though I had travelled to a different
country rather than a different island in the same country. I
greeted the Thai ladies at the reception hall of my niece's hotel
with the traditional 'wai' (hands are bought together in front of the
chin) and they just looked at me strangely, without a smile. The
usual respect for Buddha images and the Royal family were
missing from the reception of the hotel, and many of the guests of
the hotel where running around the grounds topless and openly
flirting and kissing. All the traditional values usually associated
with Thailand were completely missing from this island. I tried to
explain the difference to my niece, but she wasn't interested in
culture, as with many two week tourists, she was looking for 'a
home from home'.

Unfortunately, this is where I was involved in quite a serious back accident. If I had been in any other part of Thailand I would have had plenty of 'consideration' to help me recover, but I was in Koh Samui. My niece wanted to attend the 'full moon' party which takes place every full moon on the beaches of Koh Phang Nga which involved a speed boat ride across the short stretch of ocean. I was not that keen to go but felt obligated to my sister to keep an eye on my niece since these parties did not have a great reputation. As I looked at the speed boat being over-loaded with passengers and the rough sea conditions, I tried to talk my niece out of the trip, suspecting that this would be a very dangerous and uncomfortable boat ride. Against my better judgement and with my instinct screaming at me to turn the other way, I boarded the boat and squeezed into a standing space, all the seats already taken.

As soon as the boat gained speed it would leap off the crest of a wave and slam down into the trough of the next. This made for an uncomfortable ride for everyone, but for me, with a weak back, it was really serious. I screamed in pain as the boat slammed into the waves sending shock waves down my spine and begged for the boat to slow down. Everyone just stared at me but no one would help. I grabbed a tall American tourist and held onto him in the hope his body would take some of the impact from me, and although he was really nice, he was a bit shocked by this woman who clung to him.

By the time the boat reached the beach my back was having violent spasms and I was in extreme pain. I couldn't move but they wanted me off the boat so I was 'man-handled' by some travellers whilst some others rushed to the first aid station on the island for help. A make-shift stretcher carried me to the first-aid station where a doctor prodded me and then gave me an injection for pain. They were too scared to move me and I tried to explain to them that I needed to rest to try and stop the spasm.

I spent the night in the 'hospital' and an ambulance was organised for the following day to 'ferry' me back across to Koh Samui where they had a better hospital. This hospital fitted me with a back brace and gave me more pain killers; they didn't even take an x-ray. I had spoilt my niece's holiday and she wasn't about to spend the remainder of the holiday baby-sitting her Aunty. She found me a reasonable comfortable bungalow, not too near to her luxury hotel, and left me there to fend for myself.

I spent the next two weeks in bed, forcing myself to walk across to the restaurant once a day to try and force a meal down me and buy water. No one helped, no one came to check on me or assist me, and no one wanted the nuisance of a disabled traveller to spoil their two week holiday. One waiter took pity on me and helped me back to my bungalow one evening, only to be told the next day by him that he had been disciplined for leaving the restaurant whilst on duty (this is SO unlike Thai people). Everyday when I visited the restaurant, I called into the internet café opposite and emailed everyone I knew to come and help me.

I met an English woman called Jo who had a small business in Koh Samui, a gift shop with a yoga studio on the roof, and she befriended me and helped with my recovery. If it hadn't been for her, it could have taken much longer because I was in a downward spiral. I met up with Leanne and her mother who I travelled with in Lao, and she arranged to meet me on Koh Phang Nga for some relaxation and recovery time which really helped with the healing process. Thanks to these 3 women I eventually healed enough to travel back to Bangkok and decide my next move.

In Bangkok I booked myself into the white lodge hotel for $10 a day, much more than my budget, but my travels were coming to an end and I needed the comfort of a nice bed, private shower and fan. I spent many days in the room with a bottle of Mae Song whiskey and a packet of cigarettes for company, contemplating my next move. I had gained a lot of self-confidence and so I was happy to travel on the sky train alone and go and see some of the sights I missed last time I was in Bangkok.

The Grand Palace is an incredible sight, although I wished I had someone to share it with, ooing and aahing to yourself doesn't have the same impact. The complex was established in 1782 and it houses the royal residence, throne halls and a number of government offices, as well as the renowned Temple of the Emerald Buddha. The Emerald Buddha is in fact carved from a block of green jade and was first discovered in 1434 in a Stupa in Chiang Rai. At that time the image was covered with plaster and was thought to be an ordinary Buddha image. Later, the abbot who had found the image noticed that the plaster on the nose had flaked off, revealing the green stone underneath.

The walls of the ordination hall are decorated with mural paintings depicting several events of the Lord Buddha's life, including scenes from his birth, childhood and youth.

The Upper Terrace has four main monuments, a golden chedi; the Mondop, a repository for Buddhist sacred scriptures inscribed on palm leaves, contained within a beautiful mother-of-pearl inlaid cabinet; a miniature Angkor Wat, and the Royal Pantheon in which statues of past sovereigns of the ruling Chakri dynasty are enshrined. Scattered around the terrace are statues of elephants and mythical beings. All the other subsidiary buildings and Galleries are equally splendid and extravagant with their decorated spires and golden roofs. I was happy I had spent a good portion of my travelling budget on a new digital camera to capture the pure elegance and distinction of the palace. That is, until it was stolen.

I had enjoyed my trip to the Royal Palace and decided to visit the nearby market place for a barbecue chicken and cool drink. Whilst I was sitting down enjoying my meal, an old lady came and sat next to me and smiled. I had my bag next to my lap and didn't even consider it was at risk at all, so I didn't even pay much attention to the old lady sitting next to me. I later went into my bag to get my camera to take a picture of the river boats and was confused when I couldn't find it.

I went to the information counter at the ferry terminal and asked them if anyone had handed in a camera, I couldn't imagine where I could have left it. The Thai gentleman at the counter laughed and said it was stolen. I was astounded and told him it couldn't be stolen, Thai people don't steal! He felt so sorry for me he comforted me as I burst into tears defending his people telling him stories of how Thai people returned things to careless farangs, they didn't steal! He sadly told me that theft was common near the royal palace because of the number of tourists that visited the area. Everything I ever believed for two years about the Thai people was now being questioned again. That kind Thai man escorted me back to my hotel room, I think he understood the significance of the event, it wasn't just the theft of the camera, it

138

was a change in the Thai culture influenced by western consumerism.

I was seriously considering leaving South East Asia now, so all I had to do was decide, where exactly in the world I was going to go next. I spent the next few days around the hotel and met a group of Canadians who were travelling together from Vancouver Island. They invited me to join them on a trip to the floating market which I readily accepted as I was glad of the company and always wanted to visit the Klongs (canals).
 Bangkok was once dubbed the Venice of the East, with hundreds of miles of klongs (canals) snaking through the city. These klongs ensure the continuation of a riverine tradition that dates back centuries ago and the bustling floating market of multi-coloured boats loaded with spices and fruits and vegetables is certainly a vibrant, awe-inspiring sight.

I was invited to dinner with the Canadians and I used the opportunity to question them about Vancouver Island where most of them lived. It occurred to me I had never visited that side of the world and it might be an interesting place to visit. I had a Welsh friend who was living in Nanaimo on Vancouver Island who I had met through a cruising web site, and she said I could stay with her for a few days if I was ever to visit, so that option was looking more attractive.

I spent the next few days emailing and doing a little research into Vancouver Island, I was expecting my share of Khulula soon, which would give me a start in a new country. It never really occurred to me that I couldn't stay in Canada longer than 6 months because I had never made a plan longer than that in the last 4 years.

One of the temples in Angkor Wat

Jungle Temple at Angkor Wat

Katherine at Angkor Wat

The Angkor site covers over 77 square miles of temples, many
dating back to the 10th century and tangled in jungle roots

Stilted bamboo houses on the River Basccac

Cambodian girls selling to tourists to learn English
Girls like this now benefit from the sale of this book

Chapter 9 – Back to the First World

"The world breaks everyone, and afterward many are strong in the broken places"
Ernest Hemingway

Now that I had completed my 'loop' of Indo-china, it was time to decide if I was going to continue travelling, return to England, or do something else. I had learnt a lot about me, most of which made me feel lucky and fortunate to be given the opportunities in life that many don't get because of their circumstances. The world really was my oyster with my education and background, so I decided I should make the most of my freedom and flexibility and keep going. Opportunity knocks if you're open to it so it didn't really matter which country I visited, I just decided I should follow my instincts and let life make its own choices.

I had already considered Canada, mostly due to the many Canadian backpackers I'd met who were always such nice friendly people. These people helped me make the decision to go there, simply through their kindness to me. I'd spent 10 days mostly locked in my hotel room in Bangkok, brooding over my future, and their intervention guided my way. Once I had decided to fly to Vancouver, it was easy to go into the travel agents close to the hotel and book the flight.

My flight was via Singapore and so I decided this was also a great opportunity to give up smoking. I figured if I was going to start a new life in a new country I should reinvent myself a little and starting as a non-smoker seemed like a good beginning (also thanks to those Canadians who made it clear smoking on that side of the continent was not a good thing to do).

When I arrived at Singapore airport I had quite a few hours before my connecting flight to Vancouver so I decided to visit the transit hotel which had a wonderful swimming pool and Jacuzzi and bar on the rooftop of the airport. I don't know why more international airports don't offer these kinds of facilities to make transit flights more enjoyable. The transit hotel can be booked by the hour and has all the facilities you need to relax such as TV, bath and comfortable bed. I decided to check out the leisure facilities but couldn't find my swimming costume, not to be put-off by a small

143

problem I grabbed my sarong and decided to wear that in the pool. It was really magnificent to be sitting in a Jacuzzi staring up at the evening stars on the roof of an airport!

I strolled to the pool bar and started to chat with a South African who was on the way to Dubai. "I'd decided to give up smoking thinking this was a smoke-free airport and here I am sitting at a roof top bar watching everyone else smoke!"
"I know how you feel", he replied, "I decided to do the same so I'm suffering too"
"How about we split a packet of cigarettes and celebrate them as our last?"
"Can't think of a better way to give up smoking than to chain-smoke", he replied.

It was a great way to give up smoking; we chain-smoked so many cigarettes in a couple of hours I didn't want to face another cigarette before I got on the plane. It was also a great way to kill a few hours swapping travel stories. He found it incredible that I was flying to Vancouver to start a new life in a country I'd never visited before and yet he was off to Dubai to work in a country he'd never visited, so I didn't see the difference.

The twelve hour flight was uneventful, after spending more than twelve hours on buses and trains for the last 6 months, this journey seemed quite insignificant and quite comfortable in comparison! I kept trying to work out why I wasn't apprehensive or worried about my future so I just figured I must be doing the right thing. I had the usual questions at the airport, that you get when you have so many stamps in your passport, and then made my way to the ferry terminal for the ferry ride to Vancouver Island. I had already arranged for someone to meet me at the terminal at Duke Point and Roy recognised me by my backpack and suntan!

Arriving at Newcastle Marina in Nanaimo felt really good. I was overwhelmed by the scenery on the ferry with the snow capped mountains and the rich green forest canopy. It felt really great to breathe in the fresh crisp air of the mountains and to feel cool for the first time in years! Everyone seemed to be smiling and very welcoming to me considering they had only ever met me through the internet. Although it was February and I felt cold, the sky was a magnificent blue and the sun was shining, it was nice to feel the sun warm your skin instead of burning it. I had spent the last four years running from the sun and trying to avoid the heat and now I was bathing in the welcoming warmth of it on my skin against the cool air. It felt good to be back in the marina environment and the extraordinary kind of people who lived on boats.

My first few days seemed to be a constant round of introductions and celebrations including 3 boats which decided to go out to one of the nearby islands for a spontaneous picnic cruise in the February sunshine. I went as crew to Roy, who picked me up at the ferry terminal, on his 45 foot sail boat. Greg, went on his sailboat Seafire, which was berthed next to Alexis, and Alexis took her West coast motor boat, Lois B, that I was staying on. We rafted the boats together just off Newcastle Island and enjoyed the weekend together with several bottles of red wine.

I was immediately attracted to Greg, probably because he was so relaxed and comfortable with living on a sail boat in a marina, and he made a point to sit close to me the whole time. Greg invited me back to his boat for more red wine and we chatted at length about the cruising life and his dreams to set off in Seafire. We saw a kindred spirit in each other and we laughed until the small hours of the morning. Things started to hot up and before I knew it I was crawling into the v-berth and waking in the morning with a very large smile on my face! Greg had to go to work the next day so he left me with instructions to make myself at home and bring my bags across from next door if I wanted! I guess I never really left after that. I felt so comfortable in his presence and we fitted well together in the small confined space of his 34ft yacht. A whirlwind romance began and we started to make plans for our future together on Seafire. It just seemed like it was meant to be.

Greg was planning to take Seafire down to Mexico and invited me along. His plan was another two years working to pay off the boat and cash in his pension but I suggested we cut that to 6 months since that was as long as I could stay in Canada. I decided to invest my share of Khulula in Seafire and preparations began to get Seafire ready for the passage and tie up Greg's loose ends.

Vancouver Island is a paradise of glorious west coast scenery with lush emerald forests, alpine peaks, freshwater lakes and rivers, rocky shorelines and dazzling beaches. I wanted to see it all and balanced working on the boat and visiting as much of the island as possible. The rugged wilderness and old-growth forests provided

145

plenty of vigorous hiking that I'd been missing out on in the hotter climates, and the city of Nanaimo was a delight of attractions with its many harbour side walks and farmers markets. Pristine wilderness and wide-open spaces, rolling green landscapes of hills and valleys, forests and farmland, sparkling lakes and crystal clear rivers, all so different from the landscape I had been living in for the last four and a half years.

Diary Excerpt 31st March 2003

Cathedral Grove, McMillan Park, Vancouver Island

Today I stood under an 800 year old Douglas fir which measured 250 feet high and 30 ft in circumference. This old growth forest was so arresting with Spanish moss drenching the branches and blanketing the ancient trunks giving it an eerie ambience. It reminded me of the rain forests of Malaysia but the trees were so much more imposing in statue and I was really enjoying hiking in a much cooler climate. I just adore hiking with Greg because he is so engrossed in his environment and it's captivating to see such a beautiful rugged wilderness. As we walk and inhale the smells and sounds of the forest he constantly stops to take in another nature pleasure, bending to smell the wild rose, crouching to look closer at the mushrooms and stopping suddenly to listen more carefully to the call of a bird. It was as though my own awareness of nature was enhanced by his awareness and before long I became more observant of our surroundings, pointing at the eagle soaring in the air and the heron waiting patiently for his fish. My eyes were opened even wider to the beauty of nature in his presence. I had never experienced this with any other hiking partner before and even travelling in Asia I struggled to find this quality in many other people. Greg was a rare bird indeed.

Greg's job as a technician meant he was on the road and he often surprised me by nipping back to the marina during the day to take me on a little trip.

"I have to go to Duncan on call, I have to drive through some wonderful countryside to get there and pass through Chemainus on the way, want to keep me company?"
 "Now that's a silly question!" I smiled, "or I could just stay here and paint the deck!"

146

Duncan is known as a hub for North America Indians and has several extraordinary galleries specialising in fine First Nations Art. Chemainus is world-renowned for its more than thirty colossal, outdoor murals, making the town one massive art gallery. We visited a breathtaking river north of Duncan, called Cowichan River, with Greg's nephew, Matthew, and inhaled the pure majesty of this area. We stood on the bridge and looked down into the cobalt clear water which tumbled between mammoth boulders and saw several people sunbathing on the rocks and cooling off in the water. We took a trail down to an area where we could walk down to a small beach with vast boulders and slipped into the cool water. The day was so warm we stayed in the water for some time letting the currents sweep us down stream and into little pools caused by the eddies.

Diary excerpt 22nd April 2003

I had one of the greatest birthdays, the sun shone and Greg took me to this astonishing site on the top of a rock bluff. Standing in the sun close to the rim of a sheer rock face, the view was magnificent. Blankets of Firs with the tallest tree branches close enough to touch (or so it seemed), with the backdrop of snow-capped mountains. This country is so beautiful, and the spring is enchanting (that is, when it stops raining!). I love to inhale the blossom trees, the Magnolias in full bloom and the diverse wild flowers which seem to grow everywhere. The woodlands are carpeted with tiny blue and pink flowers and look charming. The beaches are ideal for beach-combing with their fascinating knurled drift wood and vibrant starfish which are washed ashore. I don't think I've ever seen such brilliant stout starfish, a dramatic lilac and a subtle cerise, really delightful! The spring is contagious; everyone smiles and has a spring in their step.

Love is very much in the air, very much. I feel like I have a warm glow inside. I love the dogwoods, massive perfect flowers which layer the entire tree and Frisbee golf, which I watched families play in the park (instead of a hole in the ground there is a pole surrounded by a basket that you are suppose to throw the Frisbee at and it should land into the basket). The parks are covered with magnolia and dogwood blossoms and have cool babbling rivers flowing through them. I love the call of the sea lions (I've never seen so many), and the Canada Geese that let me feed them by

*hand when they visit the marina. I love the fact I've had fresh
flowers to look at for the last two weeks, and I love the fact I smile
all the time again. If only I could be motivated to work harder
towards cruising in September!*

It's true that I was very happy with my life right now; I was putting
on weight again after losing my appetite in Asia and filling out in all
the wrong places under the influence of luxury food items Greg
kept feeding me, like fillet steak, fresh salmon and fresh cream
cakes!

I had my very own pet goose who visited me daily now so I could
hand feed her from the dock, and everyone told me she was likely
to bring her babies once they were born to visit me also. I was a
very contented cheerful woman, the only problem being I was not
allowed to stay in this seventh heaven longer than September.

The contrast of the countryside compared to where I had been
living before and the reminder of the beauty of the seasons (which
I didn't think I had missed in Asia and Africa) gave me a fresh
outlook about living in a hot climate country again.

Diary excerpt 20th May 2003

*I am so very happy and contented. A wonderful long holiday
weekend to commemorate Victoria Day in British Columbia and
what better way to celebrate than to anchor out in the bay and
watch the fantastic fireworks display from the boat. The mood in
town was magical with parades and bands and market stalls.*

We also visited the city of Victoria which is the provincial capital
and called the city of flowers, with graceful sophisticated heritage
buildings and vibrant harbour side walks complete with artists and
performers in the street to keep you entertained. The buildings
reminded me of England and the gardens were all perfectly
manicured, just like home! The imposing Empress Hotel is
legendary for 'English teas' and the striking architecture of the
building was exceptionally impressive. The historical legislative
building was especially striking in the evening when it was lit by
thousands of lights which reflected in the harbour waters. I really
loved Victoria and I commented at the time it would be a lovely
place to live with its warm climate all year round.

Greg at Newcastle Marina, Nanaimo, B.C.

Vancouver Island, B.C. A paradise of glorious west coast scenery
with lush emerald forests, alpine peaks, freshwater lakes and
rivers and pristine beaches and rocky shorelines.

Enjoying the dogwood flowers of spring on Vancouver Island, B.C.

Diary excerpt: 1st July 2003

We visited the high alpine areas of Mount Washington and Forbidden Plateau which had incredible scenery even though there was only a little snow at this time of year. The ski resort was shut down for the summer but there was a slight snow covering we could play in.

It would have been really pleasant to take the ski-lift to the top to get the view, but of course it was not operating. We walked a little way, but it would have been a stiff hike to the top where I can only imagine the 360 degree view would have been spectacular!

My pet goose wasn't spooked by our absence and she was back this morning, honking for my attention so I would go and feed her and her babies; I'm getting quite attached to them all! She surprised me the other day by turning up with two families of babies just as we were motoring out of the berth, so Greg let the boat drift whilst we fed the babies and took photos. I really look forward to the daily visit of the babies which all take on their own individual personalities and let me feed them by hand. We joked that when we leave the marina maybe the Geese would follow us in formation to Mexico!

Work was progressing on the boat and we had managed to find a second hand Aries wind vane advertised which we were going to pick up from a yacht which was sailing to the West coast. This reputable wind vane would give us an 'auto-pilot' when the boat was sailing and works with an external rudder which is bolted to the rear of the boat and is operated with a 'vane' which reacts to the wind direction. (I made it quite clear I wouldn't be hand-steering a sailing boat across a major ocean again!).

We drove across to Ucluelet across stunning country and headed for Long Beach, aptly named for its great length of perfect sand beach. The west coast is open to the Pacific Ocean and tons of driftwood ends up on the beach, from as far a field as Japan. The beach is piled high above the tide line with heaps of remarkable shaped driftwood which the local children build into interesting hides and shelters. The local artists often pick through the piles to find inspiration for their art.

We took the trail which led us along the rocky shoreline and watched the Pacific Ocean crashing onto the rocks. The tide pools were crystal clear with intense emerald green sea anemones and vibrant starfish of amethyst and cerise, sitting in a perfect aquarium garden. We took countless photographs of the many vibrant coral gardens which were formed in the abundant rock pools. We laughed at the 'beetle-head' seaweed which stood rigid in rows on the rocks and then bowed their heads into the waves as the water crashed over them. As the water retreated the 'pop stars' flicked back their hair-dos and shoke the water off them. I had never seen seaweed with such shaggy hair do's and I was fascinated by the way they danced with the movement of the water.

Time was moving on and we decided to use up Greg's holiday allowance to visit his family in Calgary, to introduce me and say goodbye! The drive across to Calgary would take us through the Canadian Rockies and the National Parks of Jasper, Banff, Glacier and Yoho, so we planned a circular return route and packed the camping gear.

Diary excerpt

The first chance I've had since leaving Vancouver, to take my eyes off the inconceivable panorama we've been driving through. The Canadian Rockies are so dramatic, almost a visual over-load with your eyes feasting on glorious vistas in every direction.

Glacier National Park

Glacier National Park sports extravagant jagged peaks with frozen rivers slowly blanketing the slopes. Each park has its own distinctive splendour, our first camp ground nestled at the base of Mount Begbie, the beginning of many impressive glaciers to come. The campsites provide all you need for a comfortable night, a private area nestled in the trees with its own fire-pit and wood and picnic table.

The following day we took a leisurely drive through Glacier National Park, relentlessly oohing and exclaiming loud wow's all the way. Simply magnificent peaks topped with glaciers thousands of year's old, substantial aged ice probably never touched. The exhibit at Roger's Pass information centre had a fascinating aariel photograph you could look at giving you a three dimensional view looking deep down into the valley and the road we had just travelled on.

Yoho National Park

Yoho National Park is known as the land of rock walls and waterfalls. Yoho is a Cree expression of awe and wonder, which describes this whole area very well. Takakkawa Falls is accessed by the 13 kilometre Yoho Valley Road which climbs precipitously and has tight sharp switchbacks all the way up. The road had only been open two weeks and we stopped on the way down for a snow ball fight. Icy cold glacier snow had melted back from the road and cooled down our hot bodies which were cooking in 34c.

The waterfalls were really glorious, tumbling from a vast height and you could climb right to the base (or all the way to the top if you wanted an icy cold shower from the spray). The river that flows from the falls is the colour of ice, the glacier melt from a glacier lake, nestled behind the summit of the mountain. The outlook from the base of the waterfall truly is awe-inspiring, jagged glacier peaks, Glacier Rivers plummeting through Alpine pines and wild flowers and a bright azure sky, quite perfect.

It makes you feel so lucky to be able to appreciate such inconceivable natural un-spoilt splendour. I guess I was particularly impressed because I had never seen a Glacier before and I found them just fascinating. I guess the price you pay for living in hot countries for too long is a profound need for anything cool!

Our camp site that night had a splendid view of the glacier and we sat around our camp fire watching the altered luminosity play on the mountains and the glacier. Our two person tent was cosy and we cuddled together on our inflatable mattress warm and toasty under our comforter.

One of the many scenic campsites in the Canadian Rockies

Bow Valley Parkway

The next day we took the Bow Valley Parkway, stopping along the way to enjoy the giant elk feeding on the wild grasses and posturing for the camera in the tumbling mountain stream. We also spotted three black bears including a baby who still had his downy baby hair and was very contented frolicking in the long

153

grasses by the road side, oblivious to his onlookers taking photographs.

Many mischievous ground squirrels sat on their hind legs amongst the smorgasbord of wild flowers and were very happy to be hand-fed by the passers by. It was a real novelty for me to see so many animals in the wild and it reminded me again of some of the things I had been missing out on. We camped at the base of Castle Mountain with its remarkable rocky turrets and close to Johnstone Canyon.

Fields of wild flowers and alpine peaks at Bow Valley Parkway

Johnstone Canyon

Boardwalks cling to the side of the canyon following the natural contours of the rock-face and give inconceivable views right into the interior of the canyon. The arresting pristine aquamarine waters that plummet down from the lower and upper falls carves amazing shapes and colours into the rock walls of the canyon giving an ever-changing vision as the water cascaded around large rocks gnarled by the water. We walked through the canyon on board walks and bridges until we reached the upper-falls which thundered down a sheer rock face framed by a striking rainbow. We chilled ourselves in the cool spray before ascending back down to see the canyon once again with a lower sun.

154

Calgary

We spent two days in Calgary, a stark disparity of flat lands and city. We celebrated Canada Day alongside the river with Greg's mum and sister and enjoyed the festive spirit of the fete. The following day we hired an inflatable boat with Greg's brother, Steve, to drift down the Bow River which flows right through the city and gives a unique view of the city sky line. As usual for this part of the world the weather can change fast and what started out to be shorts and bikini weather soon turned to hail stones and an icy wind. We stood for some time watching the clouds move and darken but decided to risk launching anyway. Within five minutes of drifting down the river, the wind suddenly picked up and skewed the raft sideways as well as picking up the speed. We rowed frantically towards an island and made land fall just as the icy rain began to fall. We made a camp-fire with the twigs and fallen wood and stood drinking bottle beer and warming ourselves on the small flames as hefty icy hale stones bounced off the shoulders of our life jackets. The distraction of keeping the fire alive and drinking beer meant we could simply wait for the storm to pass before continuing our trip down the stream. It certainly was the nicest way to view the city and very pleasurable!

The following day we said our goodbyes to family and headed for Lake Louise. The weather had become quite overcast compared to the hot sunny days we started this trip with and the lake was not displaying its full glory of bright opaque colours without the sun. The odd slash of sunlight reflected off the water giving a breath-taking sneak at the famous colours of this lake, only making you long for more.

Ice fields Parkway

Heading out along the Ice fields Parkway the weather seemed to get more over-cast and the tops of Rocky Mountains were shrouded in cloud. Peaking out just to tease you were the edges of the Ice fields which flowed from the peaks. We looked down into Peyto Lake, which is probably one of the most photographed sites for holiday brochures. The turquoise lake was nestled in a perfect valley of Alpine flowers and pine trees with a backcloth of the Rocky Mountains. Our next stop along this incredible Parkway was Mistaya Canyon, a breath-taking vista of the Bow River

155

cascading through a constricted canyon carving improbable shapes into the rocks as it gushes through the narrow gap. The alpine flowers and meadows alongside the river kept us occupied for over an hour and I couldn't resist the temptation to pocket some of the vibrantly painted patterned pebbles which created a multi-coloured border to the river. I was enthralled by these canyons. Perfectly smooth rounded potholes peppered the top of the canyon walls which in themselves were engraved into smooth curves and swirls, constantly being eroded by the cascading water. We still planned to walk the Columbia Ice field so we grudgingly left this little piece of dreamland.

Takakkawa falls at Yoho National Park

The Athabasca Glacier can be accessed from the road, and you can hike up a steep trial to the bottom of the Glacier and walk on the ice. In some places the ice is as thick as 30 stories high, but we hiked only a short distance against a sharp frosty breeze blowing off the top. We walked against the icy wind which took your breath away despite being dressed up warmly. It stung any exposed parts of skin, like the face, which were not covered. We turned around, treading carefully so as not to slip on the ice and put the freezing wind behind us.

"I visited this same glacier fifteen years ago and it has receded so drastically since then, it's like visiting a different site." Greg said. Indeed, as you walk up to the beginning of the ice field you hike pass markers which used to mark the outside edge of the glacier. Greg pointed to a mark which was nearly a mile from the edge of the ice.

"This is where I walked to when I last visited. At this point of the mountain it took a sheer drop and you could look into the ice but couldn't get onto the top to walk on it, so it was like looking through a frozen waterfall".

"I guess it looked more spectacular then, than it does now" I replied.

"Yes, it was more impressive because you were looking through the glacier rather than walking on top which is what we did".

Cold and hungry we headed for our camp site for the night and planned our last day..

Johnstone Canyon

Our final visit was to Mount Edith Cavell which was reached by a 14.5 kilometre precipitous switchback road which gave incredible views of the valley as you climb through the clouds. At the peak there is a beautiful trail which takes you right to the base of the

Cavell glacier where you can touch the 50 feet cliffs of ice and stand on the periphery of the Glacier Lake and watch the ice floes fall off and float in the lake. The solid ice cliffs are a dazzling intense sapphire within and the lake an icy azure blue. My fascination with the glaciers made me promise to visit Alaska one day with Greg and see them in their real glory.

Our final night of camping marked a drastic change in the weather and we woke to sodden bedding after a continuous night of rain. It was a reminder that we were lucky to experience such nice weather for this camping trip. We were forced to spend the last night in a motel, our wet gear stuffed into the back of the car, we were so glad this didn't happen at the beginning of our trip! I guess that is the problem with camping in these areas, once it gets wet, it stays wet, unless you happen to be lucky enough to experience as much sunny weather as we got! We were glad to get back to the marina and the comfort of Seafire.

It was a timely reminder that winter would arrive quickly and we should start making progress down the Pacific Coast of Washington and Oregon before it set in. Greg had a few more weeks at work and then the work would really notch up to get ready for cruising. One of the biggest jobs we had still to do was the provisioning for the trip and we were taking several visits to Costco each weekend to stock up on the cans and bulk foods. We were not sure of our plans but we were prepared to be at sea for several weeks if necessary and the weather was good enough. At this stage we still planned to head directly for Mexico, perhaps making Isle San Martin our first landfall, but not checking in to the country until we reached La Paz. We had purchased several cruising guides and large scale maps from another yacht who had cruised the area and we spent some time with him learning about the area and the various anchorages available.

Heading to Mexico

Diary excerpt September 1st 2003

Anchored off Sidney Spit, Victoria, finally en-route to Mexico! The first couple of days away from the marina have taught us both valuable lessons. Neither of us had actually sailed for over a year and I was astonished how nervous I was! Things soon settled down and yesterday we started to work well as a team as we

158

tacked down the channel with the rail close to the water and reaching up to five knots. It was a good test for Seafire and for us.

September 2nd 2003

A really pretty anchorage in Becher Bay, we motored up here from Oak Bay with no wind but a charming sunny day looking across Juan De Fuca Strait to the mountains of the USA. The wind is bitter cold and the water is freezing, the closer we get to the Pacific the cooler it seems, although the sun is still hot. We anchored behind three little rocky islands all by ourselves and went off exploring by dinghy the spectacular little coves in the almost tropical bay. We keep seeing lots of curious seals, so cute the way they bob their heads out of the water and look at you as if to say "what are you doing in my kitchen?" Yesterday as we left Oak Bay and visited the customs dock, a beautiful grey seal was begging for food and we could clearly see him playing in the transparent water.

As we passed Race Rocks before entering Becher Bay we spied all the loud sea lions on the islands barking their song. We'll have to move soon to a different anchorage because our little paradise is getting a little choppy and the wind is due to pick up so we need to head for Murder Bay where some civilisation and a couple of boats are anchored. That evening the wind died down again and we watched a family of sea otters playing rough and tumble and feasting on fish as the sun went down. We decided to stay the night and planned to depart for Port Renfrew as early as possible.

7th September 2003

We've been 'socked in' at Sooke Basin for three days now. We cleared Becher Bay by 7 a.m. with no wind and immediately hit a current going against us. Within an hour and still no wind, we were bashing into a south west swell as high as six feet achieving less than 2 knots over ground. As we spotted Sooke Bay from the water, the swell started to increase in size even more and we were climbing up the crest of the sharp waves then splashing down, effectively stopping the boat and achieving little more than a knot in speed overall.

We decided to take shelter in Sooke Basin since this was the last available shelter on this coastline. The first evening the wind

159

picked up as the forecast predicted 25 knots from the west (the direction we wanted to go so no good for sailing!). The following day a fog bank moved in bringing with it a bitter cold wind, so we decided to take a trip into the nearest town.

We followed the 'Galloping Goose' trial which a nice old lady told us went straight downtown (not). We detoured out of our way two and half kilometres before getting a lift from a nice old gent who dropped us off right down town and gave us instructions how to get the bus back! We exchanged money (now we were talking about calling in at some USA ports), did a little shopping for more fresh produce, and walked back out into the street into a thick fog bank. The icy fog shrouded the little town and it was quite a sight to see so much bare flesh dressed for summer suddenly assaulted by the cold fog. Back in the anchorage our boat sat underneath a sunny break in the fog bank giving us a window out of the wind and fog to work on the boat.

The weather seems to have turned quite suddenly with gales up to 30 knots featured frequently in the weather forecast and lots of fog.
"I'm worried that this is a trend which will continue, should we 'hang around' for a window or do you think it will get worse? I asked Greg.
"The news from the Pacific is not good either with South East winds up to Tuesday which would put the wind on the nose. I was looking forward to some nice down wind sailing but it's been like this ever since we started listening to the forecasts. I don't know if it's going to change", replied Greg worriedly.

September 11th 2003

We woke Tuesday morning to the wind blowing a different direction across the basin and quickly turned to the weather forecast to hear 10-15 knots from the East, just what we needed to get to the mouth of the strait! We made the quick decision to sail as soon as possible and quickly got the boat ready to head for either Neah Bay (USA) or the original plan, Port Renfrew, with little shelter. We weighed anchor at 12.45pm and arrived in Port Renfrew at 10.30 p.m. We did a little sailing to start and then had to motor the rest of the way, entering the bay with a full moon and using the radar to anchor off the beach.

It was a very uncomfortable night with the swell coming straight into the bay and hitting us beam-on, rocking the boat all night. The sound of the waves smashing on the nearby rocks didn't help either, your imagination playing games. By the following morning the fog had moved in to completely engulf us and we were socked in again, but this time in a relatively un-sheltered anchorage! We had to spend another evening there but were quick to put an optimistic ear to the weather forecast the next day. We motored out of the bay and stayed optimistic for a wind change, eventually being forced to run off-course to sail against the increasing swell to Neah Bay.

Our first gale, off Cape Flattery

The winds continued to gain strength from the west and the swells got higher. We didn't make the clearance of the rocks on our first tack and decided it was too risky to cross between the islands and rocks off Cape Flattery, so tacked again. This area had appalling seas, confused steep waves and currents which literally 'boiled' the water. Things started to go really wrong when we were forced to tack again back towards the Canadian side and the wind continued to pick up speed. The swell got bigger and steeper and we were really over-canvassed and heeling right over with the rail in the water. Greg was physically sick after trying to reduce sail and suffering from the pitching from the bow, and I was desperately holding onto a sheet (the rope that controls the sail), waiting for things to calm down a bit so I could try and get the head sail down. Greg was hanging onto the helm, retching into the cockpit and looking really ashen and my sheet started to get horribly tangled and thrashed around held only by one stopper knot.

" We have to get that sail down and it will have to be you, I can't control this sickness every time I go on the bow, and you can't control the tiller with these waves, it's taking all my strength to stop the boat from slewing." cried Greg as the boat pitched violently.
I crabbed across the deck clipped on with my safety line and collapsed onto my hands and knees on the bow of the boat timing the movement of the boat to reach up and pull the sail down. With my body as low as possible I reached up with my arms and made several timed attempts to get all the sail down and tied off. I

161

needed one hand to hold onto the boat as the bow of the boat nosed into the waves soaking me with green water and throwing me upwards as the boat slammed into the next wave. By the time I got back to the cockpit I was violently shaking with fright and hyperventilating through sheer panic. Greg was fighting with the helm trying to keep the boat from slewing sideways in the steep seas and we both heard a really loud bang indicating something was really wrong!

"I think we hit a large kelp bed, remember the one we managed to avoid on the last tack?" I screamed, "It caught the rudder of the wind vane and it wouldn't let go, so it's sheared off instead".
We since found out that the fantastic design of the Aries wind vane had built in safety measures for such emergencies, and the bolts holding down the rig sheared off, releasing the rudder as it swung up and broke the wooden vane. Disabled, but still in-tact, it was time to run down-wind back to the shelter of Neah Bay. The timing was perfect.
"Look at the log barge, it seems to be having difficulty controlling his steerage, it's as well we're now heading away from him, you can't even see him when he goes into a trough of the waves" Greg said." I wouldn't have liked to be on a collision course with that!" We'd spotted him before the waves got so big but didn't realise he was still around.

Neah Bay – Makah Indian Reservation, USA

It was approaching midnight by the time we made the entrance to Neah Bay and the entrance proved to be difficult to navigate while you squinted into the confusing lights trying to read the pilot whilst feeling sick and tired. The wind was almost certainly a gale now, at least 35 knots and waves up to 10 feet pushing us from behind.

The wind was gusting in the bay and we struggled to get the main sail down within the limited space of the bay under limited vision! I was a physical and mental wreck, trying to keep the boat pointing into the wind so Greg could get the sail down but was petrified of running out of space convinced that the breakwater wall was much closer than it really was. My mind had closed down, I was overloaded with fright, had an immense lack of energy, extreme back pain and worried sick, and I just wanted it to stop! We eventually anchored after the second attempt and crawled into bed after spending 12 hours tacking nowhere!

September 18th 2003

Our one week anniversary in Neah Bay was celebrated with gale force winds almost identical to those we came in with! Last night it blew and blew and the wake from the swell came into the bay rocking the boat in our nice quiet bay we had got quite used to. We now have the company of another 4 yachts we think are also heading south. We met Bob and Rita on the sailing yacht Farewell who are going to be harbour hopping down the USA coast all the way to Mexico and we think we are going to take the same route, so we'll probably meet up again. A weather window of three days starts on Saturday and we're hoping we can get as far as Coos Bay before it changes again.

Neah Bay is populated by Makah Indians and the people are really friendly and smiley and they have one basic general store which is expensive but seems to stock about everything you'd need. They are quite cut-off in this furthest North West corner of the USA, so they are quite self-sufficient. They have an interesting museum with information on the First Nations and interesting artefacts.

Diary excerpt:

The area has prolific wildlife and 2 large sea lions are resident in the bay, splashing and feeding right off the dock. The water was clear enough that you could see them diving for large halibut and then jumping out of the water with the big fish in their mouths and throwing them across the water to tear a piece off. The sea gulls were going crazy scavenging off the fish before it sank and the sea lion surfaced again to feed and tear the fish apart once more. We could have watched it for hours but the wind was bitterly cold on our faces. The bay was full of screaming sea gulls which were following the seals around surfacing with fish in their mouths and throwing them across the water.

We also spotted Pelicans for the first time, Pelicans? Here? We got quite close before they all took off flying in formation, no doubt for California and warmer waters!

163

The many fishing boats at Fort Bragg Marina, Northern California, USA – we eventually anchored in the River instead.

Coos Bay, Oregan, USA – waves as high as 27 feet

Chapter 10 - USA Pacific Coast

"We all have the extraordinary coded within us, waiting to be released"
Jean Houston

We eventually left Neah Bay and rounded Cape Flattery on the 20th September. The weather forecast called for North to North East winds 5-15 knots but we didn't get any wind at all and motored out into the Pacific until sight of land disappeared with calm seas, a clear blue sky and lovely sunshine. By early morning the temperatures had plummeted to 7c but the sun started to warm us as we sailed into our second day at sea. We were optimistic of reaching California, even if we had to motor the whole way, when the weather forecast suddenly warned of high winds up to 30 knots building in our area.

We decided not to risk it and headed back towards Grays Harbour rather than Coos Bay another 30 miles south. As we approached Grays Harbour we called the Coast Guard to get the latest bar report. "This is the Yacht Seafire approaching Grays Harbour; can you please give us a current bar report?" Greg called on the VHF

"Conditions are good, have you ever crossed a bar before?" asked the Coast Guard. We hadn't and we'd heard horror stories about the bars which cross nearly all the entrances to harbours on the west coast. The bars are affected by the vast volume of water in the Pacific Ocean trying to force itself into the narrow entrance of the harbours. If you don't navigate the bars at the right tide you can get swept into tidal rips and standing waves. In anything other than calm conditions and slack tide, it can be a very dangerous crossing and so yachts are always advised to check the bar conditions before entering.
 "No Sir we have not, do you have any advice?" Greg replied.
"Would you like the Coast Guard to give you an escort as a training exercise?" It seemed like a good idea to get an escort across our first bar whilst providing real training experience for the Coast Guard, so we readily accepted.
 "Thank you we will stand by for instructions" It was interesting to watch the Coast Guard boat rush out of the bay to our 'rescue' and escort us across the bar giving us information along the way which would be invaluable to the other numerous bar crossings

we would have to make down this coastline. Once inside the bay we met up again with Yacht Farewell and Bob and Rita who came to take our lines as we came alongside the docks.

Diary excerpt 24th September

We're both still worried about the time clicking away, but don't want to be forced into weather that makes us nervous; we're determined to take our time and do day hops, next run 27 hours at 5 knots and after that we can do even shorter hops which will be a lot easier to plan weather windows.

We're both very happy and beginning to enjoy exploring new territory, taking trips ashore at the harbour towns of Washington. We had a lovely trip yesterday into the sleepy little town of Aberdeen on the local bus. Temperatures went up to 77f which cheered us proving summer was still around, although the fog is ever present.

The Sleepy harbour town of Westport, Washington, USA

We both really like Westport with its extensive ideal surfing beaches and affable people who are ever eager to help the cruisers. They really seem genuinely interested in our voyage and eager to help out in anyway. The harbour towns have a great respect for the sea and love to hear your stories and plans. The only grocery store in town even visited her local supermarket, close to her home to buy me a flat of eggs because their store didn't usually carry so many eggs. The ladies in the local souvenir store kept me talking for over an hour when I visited their store to see if I could buy a Mexican flag.

The town had a charming 'holiday' ambience and the wildlife was abundant with a troop of grey mottled seals in the bay which gave us plenty of amusement watching them fish and fool around. We also saw quite a number of Pelicans which we found enthralling to watch, as they dove from incredible heights to fish. We really enjoyed walking the breakwater wall and watching the giant 360 feet paddle boat which was en-route to San Francisco to be used as a museum. You could easily stay in this enchanting town for a longer period of time but we were preparing to leave after a week's stay when the wind was forecasted at 10 knots. We planned the next leg to Newport and hoped to move on quickly to Coos Bay and onwards to California.

Diary excerpt 30th September

Arrived in Newport yesterday afternoon after a long day and night motoring into the wind and choppy seas. I actually felt quite sea sick and was really relieved to arrive. Now we're on our way again after a 24 hour stopover. The sea is the flattest we've experienced so far, like a lake with virtually no swell and only a little wind. We sailed for the first couple of hours with a lovely down-wind position in an eerie light caused by low thin fog close to the water. If you looked up there was bright blue sky and we were trapped inside a moving halo of glassy seas and a fence of white cloud. We're both feeling really good about our southerly progress; soon we'll be in California!

We only stayed for the night at Newport and left for Coos Bay the next day to catch a good weather window. At least we would be leaving the state of Washington and entering Oregon with our next landfall. It was the best passage so far with completely flat seas and a little North wind which gave us a very comfortable passage, despite being back in a cold dense fog bank most of the way. We had to slow down because we were going to arrive too early for the bar crossing, and suddenly we lost all forward transmission. The wind had died down and we were only 14 miles off. We ghosted at 2-3 knots finally dropping our speed to as low as 1 knot, meaning it would take another 14 hours to reach the bar at Coos Bay!

 The timing for this bar was critical and so we called the Coast Guard to tell them of our intentions.

"We have lost all forward transmission and so we can not use our engine. The wind has now dropped meaning we can only make a speed of 1 knot. Our intention is to cross the bar at Coos Bay before the tide changes again and so we will sail slowly in that direction"

"Please keep in radio contact with the Coast Guard and report hourly your GPS position and speed", replied the Coast Guard. We kept this up for the next 7 hours but maintained the same speed meaning we would not make the entrance in time for the change in tide. This meant the crossing would have been dangerous with no forward transmission from our engine.

167

The coastguard called us on the VHF to get our position and speed.

"We are still 7 miles from the entrance to the harbour and we are currently making an average of 1 knot" reported Greg (for those non-sailors this is approx equivalent to 1 mile an hour, most people can actually walk a lot faster than this without even trying!)

"O.K. we would like to come out and tow you into the harbour, otherwise you will miss the slack tide and will be making a dangerous crossing against the tide with no engine."

"O.K. we will prepare the boat for a tow" replied Greg. And so, for the second time on the USA coast, the Coast Guard had helped us out in our moment of need. We were very grateful for their assistance which they again used as a training exercise. This service was provided free of charge since they preferred to take preventative safety measures rather than rescue a boat in danger. Across the bar, Yacht Farewell and Bob and Rita were ready to take our lines again and commented that the Coast Guard had once again assisted our arrival.

Charleston, Coos Bay, Oregon, USA

This harbour was a popular fishing and crabbing port and legendary for the Dungeness crabs with many weekenders visiting the port to fish or crab in the bay. There was always an interesting crowd of people and the local RV Park provided good amenities including showers, internet access and laundry. We knew we would have to stay more than two weeks here to sort out our transmission problem and so committed to a month's moorage which was cheaper than the day rate as long as you stayed longer than 14 days.

We enjoyed walking through the woodland up to the Coast Guard lookout which gave a superb view of the bar entrance.
 You could observe boats navigate the bar and when there was a 'rough bar' warning we always headed up there to see if any crabbing boats attempted the entrance. You often saw the Coast Guard cutters training in the rip tides and we even saw coast guard helicopters on training exercises simulating sea rescues in some of the worse breaking waves. We would spend hours up there looking out at the violent sea reminding ourselves why we were sitting safely in the marina.

Most of the RV's we met were also on the way down to Mexico, mostly Canadians escaping the cold winters (called snowbirds). We often joked they had a much easier journey than we were letting ourselves in for; their only concern the cost of fuel! We marvelled at these 'land yachts' that were mostly living the same 'self-sufficient' life style we were living on the sea, but without the inconvenience of the stormy weather and high winds to delay the journey! We often joked with the idea of trading in Seafire for a 'Winnebago'.

We looked up Mike who we had met in Grays Harbour and had invited us to visit him on his motor boat if we called in at Coos Bay. Mike and his wife lived on their boat in the marina and happily took us on a tour of the area. We were very appreciative for this since it gave us the opportunity to explore this craggy coastline and all it has to offer.

"We'll drive along the Cape Arago Highway which follows the coastline and head for Cape Arago lighthouse. We'll make a stop at Sunset Bay State Park for lunch and walk the sheltered beach and then head for the Oregon Coast trail to Simpson reef and Shell Island" said Mike, packing us into the back of his car.

"Simpson Reef and Shell island has astounding rock formations where the sea crashes into the shoreline and this is the breeding season for the seals and sea lions so you'll be able to watch them from the lookout", he added.

We drove through spectacular scenery and arrived at the lookout for Shell Island which is the northern-most breeding ground on the Pacific Coast for the Californian sea lion and Stellar sea lion, as well as the gigantic Elephant seal.

"It says here on the information board that the Stellar sea lion weighs up to 2000 pounds and can be as long as 10 feet and the pups are 40lb at birth", I exclaimed

"Well, the Elephant seal is the largest member of the seal family and the deepest diving mammal, reaching depths of 4000 feet and only come to land to breed and to moult" replied Greg, who was also reading off the information board. "And they weigh as much as two and a half tons and are up to 13 feet long!"

"Unfortunately you see many dead pups though", stated Mike, "the pups can not survive in the water until 8-10 weeks after birth and many of the winter storms wash waves over Shell Island knocking them into the ocean, so the pups rarely survive"

We watched all the different kinds of seals and sea lions existing together on this island; simply because it gave them the best shelter around from the storms. It looked like a carpet from a distance because every available space was taken by pups or adults. In the water nearby, the playful Harbour seal pups frolicked in the water, teasing the Elephant seal pups because they can swim at birth and are independent within three weeks. The barking from the sea lions was thunderous and we had to shout to be heard above the racket from the lookout on the road. Mike took us on a weekend trip to the Oregon Dunes which are north of Coos Bay and closer to the smaller bar crossing of Winchester Bay. This is a popular area for riding the dune buggies on the massive sand dunes and miles of continuous white sand beaches. It is a magnificent sight to see so much sand piled high with nothing else around for miles and miles. The sand is a fine chalky consistency and it reminded us of light snow, indeed from a distance the dunes could be mistaken for ski slopes. Our foot prints made the only marks on the perfect sand and we clambered up the immense dunes and could see nothing but sand as far as the eye could see. Some families bring their children to sledge on the sheer dunes but we were happy to run up and down and make 'snow angels' in the faultless sand. Nestled between the dunes was a small oasis of a little river made into a nature reserve and we had a picnic there watching the birds.

Diary excerpt October 10th

While we were waiting to receive our new transmission, the seas really grew to incredible heights, caused by a storm off Alaska. Each day more fishing boats turned up at the docks and each day the surf got higher and higher, until on Saturday they were reporting swells of 27 feet!

We visited Cape Arago with Mike who said there was a magnificent lookout on the top of the cliffs where you could watch the booming waves. The surf was crashing against the rock cliff face and the sheer capacity of water colliding with the land literally bubbled and foamed as it ran off the rocks. It reminded me of whipped milk and the detonation of the waves was like a glorious fireworks display. Greg got some extraordinary photos and I could have spent all day there just watching the waves. The cliff trail took you right along the precipice and you could watch the waves crashing all along the coastline, which had created different rock formations with the wave action. It turned into a lovely sunny day and we had a picnic in Shore Acres State Park and enjoyed the botanical gardens there. It seemed illusory that we were actually sailing this stormy coastline on our little 34 foot boat and reminded ourselves not to get caught in this kind of weather.

By the time our transmission arrived it turned November and we were still experiencing gales up to 45 knots.
Even though we were close to Northern California the temperatures had plummeted to 4c at night time and we were using our little electric heaters on the docks. We checked the weather daily and eventually a big high was predicted bringing calm weather and higher temperatures.

Diary excerpt 2nd November

We caught a great weather window of a big high which bought really high temperatures for the time of year and decided to make as far south as possible. We rounded Cape Mendocino in horrid seas with very light winds but as we passed the cape at night the wind suddenly accelerated and the autopilot alarm went off.

Cape Mendocino and 15 feet seas

The auto helm could no longer cope with the increased wind and steep seas and Greg jumped on the helm.
"We need to get down the sail, we are way overpowered and the GPS is showing a speed of 8.5 knots! We're going too fast down these steep waves and the boat is slewing all over the place!"
I remembered Cape Flattery in a flash back and there was no way I was going to crawl out onto the bowsprit (the pole that sticks way out in front of the boat which the sail is attached to) in the pitch black and take down the sail. Unfortunately there was no way I could take the helm with the heavy weather helm either, so something had to be done! The 'slewing' of the boat meant that we were cork-screwing in the water, the boat being smashed from wave to wave in all directions and being carried down the waves into a potentially dangerous wall of water.
"The seas are colossal! Those waves behind us must be 15 feet tall; it looks like a wall of water bearing down on us! Maybe we should engage the wind vane and see if that can handle the steering" I screamed.

171

"O.K. but you'll have to edge out on the boomkin at the stern while I try and keep the boat steady!"

This was still a daunting thing to do, two planks of wood extend out from the cockpit and beyond the external rudder, at the back of the boat, and suspend over the water. This is what the wind vane is attached to so I needed to scramble out over the water, gaze into the wall of water above my head and try and release a tiny pin to engage the wind vane. This then meant the 'auto-pilot' would take over as the 'vane' reacted to the wind direction and steered the boat with the external rudder.

"I think I've engaged it" I shouted back to Greg in the cockpit as I hung on for dear life as the boat pitched ferociously in the water.

"Come back here and we'll look, it's too dangerous out there!"

I had done it incorrectly and Greg explained the turning motion to engage the pin, it was a question of pulling it out and then turning it one turn clockwise, no mean feat on a pitching boat balanced on a plank of wood looking into 15 feet waves!

"O.K. I've definitely got it this time, engage the vane!"

That did the trick and the wind vane handled the seas well, keeping us on a good course and preventing the boat from slewing.

Within two hours the wind started to die down once we got away from the effects of the acceleration around the cape, and we were left with steep confused seas and a light wind. We saw the entrance for Fort Bragg as the sun was rising and considered the narrow bar entrance a cinch compared to what we had just experienced!

Fort Bragg, Northern California, USA

This was the only West Coast town where we did not receive a welcoming embrace. The boat basin was in bad repair with poor docks and facilities and yet charged a daily rate significantly higher than any other on the whole of the West coast. After four days of being on the 'wrong side' of the river for town access, we decided to risk anchoring in the River now that the tidal range was less pronounced. At low tide we only had enough depth to prevent grounding but the river was free, town was closer and the river was very peaceful. The people with the local businesses would not allow us to tie our dinghy to their docks and so we had to motor down river to the industrial area where we tied up behind a warehouse. From here we could walk up a steep hill into the delightful town and explore the whole area. There was a wonderful trail which went the length of the coastline called the 10 mile trail and the beaches off the path were craggy and striking. Glass beach was an unusual beach with smooth rounded multi-coloured glass pebbles, remnants of a glass factory which used to be close by. I collected many unusual shaped and coloured glass trinkets from this beach and was not the only one doing so!

In the meantime we listened to the weather forecast where winds were not such a problem but massive swells of 11-12 feet were reported with 3-5 feet wind waves. We didn't need 18 feet seas and so we chose to wait for them to die down. It looked like the wind was switching to the south again which was no good for us either, so we were stuck in Fort Bragg for at least another week. We heard from the Yacht Farewell that they were stuck in Crescent City, further north than us, so their fate was worst than ours. The only good news was that San Francisco should be our next stop and the weather should start getting better the further south we progressed.

Diary excerpt 7th November 2003

We decided to take off with a day weather window and the seas were really quite flat and got even better as we passed Point Arena. The wind was on the nose, which was not as forecasted, and I was concerned this indicated the gales would reach us earlier than predicted, but we arrived in Bodega Bay with an uneventful passage.

Bodega Bay, California, USA

This beautiful sheltered bay is entered by a wide bar which then turns into a narrow long channel leading into the main bay. The Bodega head trail takes you high into the hills and up to incredible cliffs with multi-coloured ice plants carpeting the ground.

Diary excerpt 9th November

Here at Bodega Bay we seem to be anchored in a bird sanctuary, so many birds I've never seen before, neat little long billed curlews with pretty light brown coats and a ridiculous outsized slender beak and the American coots that waddle along like little black chickens. In the trees sit big herons with red eyes and blue splashes on their wings, a type of heron which sometimes look like owls and sometimes an eagle through the leaves of the trees.

We also saw many types of distinctive marsh birds which we couldn't identify and lots of pelicans diving from great heights. We had a wonderful few days in Bodega and walked the whole bay area. The Bodega head trail took us high up in the hills to incredible cliffs you could look down to the rocky coastline. We did a circular route which took us past a group of large white pelicans preening themselves and a group of birdwatchers who were delighted by the sight. I was amazed by their size with a 5 foot wing span and pure snowy white. It is a rare sight to see these types of pelicans in the wild so we felt really honoured that we could watch them for quite some time. We did spot them again from our anchorage but this was the closest we ever got to them.

We also spotted ample osprey in elegant flight and plenty of turkey vultures with their distinctive bald red heads. We walked through hillsides of ice plants ranging in colour from jade and lime to ruby and crimson and spotted many deer grazing. We also came pretty close to 2 giant skunks on the trails but were careful to not upset them so they wouldn't spray! As we headed back downhill we walked through meadows of golden grasses and came across a cougar kill and then crossed the sand dunes back to the marina, completing an 8 km circle on a pleasant sunny day.

We really enjoyed ourselves and felt like we had eventually caught up with summer!

One day the wind really picked up in the bay and changed direction and we were concerned that our anchor would drag, putting our boat too close to a rocky shoreline and shallower water.

"I think we should pull up anchor and head for shelter in the marina across the way" shouted Greg, as the wind speed increased and the boat started to pitch in the swell.

"Yes, this wind is blowing from the south so it leaves the anchorage exposed to a long fetch all the way down the channel", I agreed.

We radioed the marina to request a slip and the only option was a difficult manoeuvre for our boat. We entered the marina entrance with no problems, but as we turned the boat to head down one of the narrow slips a sudden gust of wind overpowered the tiller since we were going so slowly. The boat was blown sideways and we were heading for the boats tied up to the opposite dock.

"I've lost all steerage against this wind", shouted Greg, "get ready to fend off"

Lucky for us some fellow yachties saw what was happening and threw us a long rope from the opposite dock.

"O.K. the line is secure!" I yelled from the stern, and several strong men started to pull on the rope to get our stern straight so Greg could get some steerage back.

After a few attempts we made it into the slip and sincerely thanked our rescuers!

As soon as the boat was securely tied to the dock we headed for the shower rooms and bumped into Joe who was on the way down to greet us.

175

"You've been providing a very pleasant view for me from my house while you've been anchored on the other side of the bay"
"Well thank you, and your house looks quite beautiful from the water too", we replied.
"Well, I'd wanted to invite you to dinner but I had no way to come out to you on the water, so I rushed over here as soon as I saw you heading for the marina".
"That's really kind, when did you have in mind?"
"Well I figured you guys might appreciate a lift into town and do some provisioning, there is no public transport from the bay and very few in the way of groceries around here."
"That's really kind; we did wonder how close the nearest town was"
"Well, if you're free now I'm just going to lunch in the little village nearby here where the movie 'The Birds' was filmed. I can show you the school house and church where it was shot and I'd like to treat you to lunch in a lovely little café nearby."
"Perfect, give us 30 minutes to shower and change and we'll be right with you"

This was so typical of so many people we met on the west coast of America. They were genuinely interested in our journey and our progress so far and provided lifts to the local shops or tours of their area. This must be unique to travelling by boat; I can't imagine that a couple arriving by RV or car would get the same reception. I guess it just goes to show the kindness of people when they understand you don't have your own land transport.

We were invited into Joe's home, he bought us lunch, showed us his home town, took us to all the grocery stores in the main town which was a good 40 minutes by car, and shared a bottle of very nice red wine with a home cooked meal the following evening. We swapped stories and he gave us a weather fax modulator so that we could download weather faxes onto our computer via the single sideband radio on our boat. His welcome, the yachties who helped us in the marina and the beautiful bay will stay in our memories for a long time.

Diary excerpt 14th November

We're now underway again and crossing the San Francisco Bay right now. Reyes Point Lighthouse looks really remarkable the way it is perched on a steep cliff and balanced on a small peak. It seems astonishing that we're so close to a big city when the coastline from the sea just looks like high craggy hills. Of course we can't see 'into' the bay where the city is, but it still seems incredible that there is suppose to be a big city behind those hills!

We had discussed at detail whether we should enter the bay or anchor off Drakes Bay or Half-Moon Bay and do an 'excursion' into the city. The tides and wind conditions to go under the famous San Francisco Bridge were notorious and we were eager to keep moving south, so we decided to head for Half-Moon Bay on the south side of the city.

Diary excerpt 21st November

We spent the first few days exploring the local area and found the bus service into Half-Moon Bay town and beyond. We worked out the train service and decided to visit the city.

The beautiful city of San Francisco, California, USA

The bus took a breathtaking journey across the striking hills and vineyard country of this area. It seemed unfeasible that a major city was somewhere amongst this rich green panorama but we eventually saw the buildings to indicate we were getting closer. We crossed from the bus station to the rail station and took the short service downtown to the city. Being tourist for the day, we rode the street trolley to the fishermen's wharf admiring all the handsome candy-coloured majestic buildings and the precipitous streets, just like you see in the movies! The old gent on the cable car held a microphone and told jokes and explained the history of the buildings and pointed out the views down to the bay. It seemed impracticable that cars could park on such steep hills and many of the buildings had different height doors at street level.

We watched the old trams clattering down the street on the water front and admired the view of the golden gate bridge and Alcatraz Island from the historical piers. The weather was implausible for the time of year, hot and sunny, and all the tourists were wearing shorts and t-shirts and merrily enjoying the famous San Francisco skyline view from the water. The city is striking and the architecture beautiful and very colourful. This is a city I would defiantly like to spend more time in to explore.

Diary excerpt 23rd November

The weather is not being kind to us generally. One storm system after another and we worry about safe anchorages or very expensive marinas. At Half-Moon Bay we had a safe anchorage. and yet our anchor still dragged in 30 knot winds in the Bay. It means we are stuck on the boat while the wind blows and when the wind dies down either the swells are too high or the weather window isn't long enough to run to our next anchorage. We don't think Santa Cruz will be safe now so we have to go the extra to Monterey Bay where the anchorage looks iffy for protection.

That was the case, although we stayed one night off the pier at Santa Cruz and left the next day for Monterey. We tried to anchor outside the marina breakwater but found the depth suddenly shelved and too dangerous. Whilst we were sounding the area, a gent was shouting at us down from the pier to say the marina had winter rates available and lots of space. We decided it would be safer to go into the marina and found the same man waiting for us in the marina office with a big smile. We loved Monterey. It was well worth the $144 in marina fees we had to pay, and enjoyed the festive spirit of this historical tourist town.
We played the tourist again and visited many of the English pubs (we spotted 4 in one street) and drank Boddingtons ale, ate lamb shank Sunday lunch and shopped in the many nautical shops. We even bought matching 'Monterey' Jackets for $20 in the sale and laughed when we saw every other tourist wearing the same jacket which was for sale everywhere (the weather was a little cool on days and many of the tourists were not prepared). We loved the fisherman's wharf with its many bars and cafes and holiday mood and enjoyed the sumptuous facilities of the marina which included internet, hot showers and weather faxes. We had the usual mix of nice warm sunny weather and howling gales, although it was generally protected in the bay. As soon as we had the weather window we set off for Morro Bay, leaving at 2 p.m. and arriving 9 a.m. the following morning to catch the slack tide for the bar. As soon as we entered the bar we were hailed on the VHF radio.

"Yacht Seafire this is Mike from Morro Bay, I've been expecting you for months!"
 Mike had been following our progress on our website (www.nomadaroundtheworld.com) which Greg had been updating with photos and stories from each port.
"I've been following your trip and looking forward to meeting you. We're heading the same place."
"Great, where are you, we'll come and meet you"
"I'm leaving today. I've been waiting for a good weather window to go around Point Conception and today don't look too bad. You can use my marina slip whilst you're here if you want, I'll contact the marina and tell them I'm sub-letting it to you."
It was a nice offer, but without a car it was too far away. We met Mike anyway and chatted for a short time before we helped him cast off.
"I think you'll be stuck here for a couple of weeks. I've waited for weeks before this window came along. Good luck anyway!"
"Thanks but I'm looking forward to meeting my friend who lives here!" I replied.
I had met Claire in the Cameron Highlands in Malaysia and we spent a few days together hiking in the rain forest. We had kept in email contact and she said if I was ever in Morro Bay I should look her up. She was looking forward to us getting here too so we had already planned on staying at least a week.

Morro Rock at Morro Bay, USA

Sunbathing on the sand dunes at Morro Bay.

The Bay is protected by Morro rock and we anchored in a relatively small area between the various mooring buoys in the estuary. Morro Rock is a dominant peak 580ft high, which was once underground, until volcanic activity changed the shape of the land and created an island. Today it forms one wall of the breakwater to the north, the extensive sand dunes giving shelter from the west and south and providing many hours of hiking entertainment. The estuary formed by the breakwater and Morro rock is a protected park and attracts many birds to the wetlands.

This pretty tourist town has many sights to delight the eye. We spent two delightful weeks at Morro Bay and had plenty of side excursions, thanks to Claire. She took us on many trips around the area and she loved hiking so we got the chance to see some of the amazing countryside and farmland. We visited the nearby town of San Louis Obispo and the lovely historical district with its quaint shops and cafes. The coastline of Morro Bay has many interesting rock formations and a hike provides many sights of unique caves and arches formed by the surf. We watched several

180

surfers taking advantage of the high waves and were quite surprised to see how close to the rocky shore line they were.

Diary excerpt

The dunes form an 8 mile long sand spit which protects the bay and gave us many enjoyable hours of hiking. We've seen many varieties of birds and enjoy watching the curlews bury their protracted beaks into the sand as they burrow for small worms and clams. We spend many afternoons sitting in the cockpit watching the white and brown pelicans as they dive for food and the herons who stand perfectly still, balanced on one foot, on the edge of the waterline.

The outlook from the estuary at low tide from one of the highest sand dunes gave us a charming view of the protected wetlands and the Salinas valley in the background where the water runs from.

Diary excerpt 11th December 2003

Yep! After 1100 miles of awful swell and horrid seas and wind, there are just a few hundred miles left to San Diego and then Mexico! We've met another yacht here called Scottish Mist and we may be buddy boating with them on our first adventures into Mexico. Bob and Doreen have been stuck here with engine troubles and now they are also waiting for a weather window to go around Conception.

We had a great weekend with Claire and we invited some of her friends we had met to celebrate the Christmas boat parade in the bay. Many boat owners made the effort to light up their boats with Christmas lights, some all the way up the masts and others creating sledges and reindeer models on their decks. It was a reminder that at least we had made it to California for Christmas, even though we had hoped to be in Mexico to celebrate.

That weekend we planned to hike up to the Pinnacles, but Greg had to stay with the boat since our anchor had dragged when a squall hit us at 5 a.m. that morning. Claire had arranged to meet some friends there and it was a good 2 hour drive through the Californian vineyards to get there. We didn't get there until 1p.m and by the time we met up with the friends and visited the centre to register ourselves, it was 3 p.m. before we started to hike. It was a really arduous hike to the summit of the Pinnacles which stand at 2714 feet and I was always lagging behind because of my back troubles. Several times I wanted to stop or turn back, but I could see that it was going to get dark soon and I didn't fancy trying to find my own way back to the centre. It was an unbelievable sight seeing all the absurd rocky outcrops formed by earthquakes, these Pinnacles being right on the San Andreas Fault line. The centre had warned of rock falls and everywhere you could see evidence of recent falls, and many vast boulders balanced ready to fall.

The aim was to reach the zenith for sunset and they all rushed ahead of me to try and make it in time. By the time I got there it was dusk and we started to plan the long hike down, which would inexorably be in the dark. I wasn't that happy with this situation, usually being very cautious with my footing because a fall would be very dangerous to my spine. Hazardous loose rocks and perilous paths meant this was going to be quite a difficult descent in the dark. Added to this Claire warned of Mountain Lions (Cougars) that were known to attack women and children, and bears who had the same taste! Further to that, the howling of the coyotes, and the possibility of snakes and spiders on trail, I was pretty anxious.

We made it back down in one piece, mostly in the pitch black dark, and immediately set back to Morro Bay. I said my farewells to Claire and promised to keep in touch. One week later I heard on the news that there had been a major quake in the Morro Bay area and that the Pinnacles suffered more shifts in the rock formations and some major rock slides. By this time we were in San Diego and I thanked my lucky stars it didn't occur a week earlier when I was climbing the Pinnacles!

Diary excerpt 19th December

We agonised about the right conditions to round Point Conception and decided to leave with Scottish Mist. It was well worth the wait with lovely calm weather, long swells, and a great passage. Once we got into Santa Barbara channel, the swells were really knocked down and even the night passage became an enjoyable experience! The oil rigs were lit up like Christmas trees and provided plenty of visual entertainment, and then a giant pod of dolphins and great schools of fish provided even more entertainment. The phosphorescent fish covered large patches and you could clearly see each individual fish darting in different directions and then the dolphins left trials as they chased and dived and played in the bow wave, quite a show! The sights along the coast have been amazing; right now I can see Malibu, film star mansions and swimming pools high in the mountains. We're heading directly for San Diego and should arrive around noon tomorrow. Tonight is likely to be busy with shipping, so the night will go quickly again.

We arrived in San Diego a little later than expected, just in front of a storm which we ran in front of as we entered the harbour. Scottish Mist was ahead and already tied up alongside the police dock, so we radioed for them to catch our lines as the wind had turned really gusty. Both boats secured moorage at the transient marina at the Police dock for 5 days, and we immediately started to decorate the yachts with Christmas lights to get into the festive spirit. We planned to spend Christmas day together and took advantage of the plentiful provisions available to make a special day. We spent Christmas day aboard Scottish Mist, with Bob and Doreen. We shared the cooking, bringing roast lamb and roasted potatoes and parsnips from our barbecue, and joining their roast chicken, green beans and all the dressings! Pumpkin pie and bread pudding was baked by Doreen, and we sat at a fantastic table setting complete with mini Christmas tree, fir cones and festive napkins and rings.

The view from Shelter Island where we were docked looked across San Diego Bay, with the city in the distance. Shelter Island is a beautiful area with hotels and marinas and plenty of palm trees, and we really enjoyed walking the promenade. The promenade looked out to the Bay anchorage and gave a great view of the many yachts sailing on the weekend with their colourful spinnakers. The 'Star of India' was originally built in England in the early 1900's and is now an exhibit in the city and took sailing trips around the Bay, and looked beautiful with her many sails. The island is kept so clean that even the palm fronds are cleaned up as soon as they blow off the trees! The skyline of San Diego is really attractive and they visibly spend a lot of money on public art, judging by the display of 'urban trees' along the whole of the sea front. These diverse sculptures were witty interpretations of trees, built from various materials and enthralling

183

to look at. The cruisers anchorage was close to down-town and we loved to watch the sun go down on the city and watch the orange sphere reflected on the many mirrored buildings. As soon as it turned dusk the city was ablaze with Christmas lights decorating all the skyscrapers and creating a glitter of reds, greens and gold's on the horizon.

Diary excerpt 2nd January

We explored 'downtown' taking the trolley bus on a circular tourist route and admired this stunning city. We spent New Year's Eve at the 'first night' celebrations on Shelter Island and had an extraordinary night listening to the various bands and watching the many shows. Now we're ready to go and tomorrow we plan on a final provisioning trip to 'Costco' and then 'off' to Mexico. There is a local marina called 'Downwind' who provides all kinds of information to boats taking off for Mexico and one of their perks was free use of their ancient truck to buy last minute provisions. The weather forecast is good for Monday, Tuesday, and Wednesday so with a three day window, there is nothing to stop us from setting off once we have the done the last shopping.

Unlike Bob and Doreen on Scottish Mist and a family from Canada, both who were planning to take off for Mexico at the same time as us, and both with major engine problems. The girls were in tears as we said our farewells and we hoped they could rejoin us further down the line once they had sorted out their boat problems.

Chapter 11 - Baja California, Pacific West Coast, Mexico

"You must take your chance" William Shakespeare

Diary excerpt

At last!!! Sunshine, flat seas and fantastic scenery!! We've eventually stopped at a place, just because we want to....not to wait for a weather window. We left San Diego on the 5th January, with wonderful calm weather and some of the flattest seas we've experienced. We had a lovely sail for the first few hours, doing 4 to 5kts with all 3 sails flying until the wind died down and we had to fire up the engine again! Still I wouldn't have traded those flat seas and sunshine for anything. As the day warmed up, we stripped off our long johns and realized we were probably going to be storing them away (at last). We had a divine night sail with a full moon and arrived at Isle San Martin the following afternoon
.

Isle San Martin is an extinct twin peaked volcano with a natural harbour formed by the lava flow...amazing stuff. The fishing post looked pretty run-down and the beach was strewn with litter and bottles and a new looking sail boat without a mast. We later found out that this boat was wrecked on Christmas day when it dragged anchor in 30 knot winds. Charlie's charts (a popular cruising guide for this area), does warn that this can be a dangerous anchorage in north-west winds, so we were sorry to see that someone had been caught out here, especially on Christmas Day.

We understand that there were 3 boats all celebrating together when the wind started to pick up. This boat was anchored closest to the rocks near the beach and they couldn't get their anchor up in time to escape to the safer anchorage on the other side of the island. The other boats were busy getting their own anchors up and saving themselves and by the time they had re-anchored safely, the other boat had already been blown into the rocks. They were in contact via VHF radio the whole time but couldn't do anything to help, looking after their own safety first. They launched a rescue mission with their dinghies (a dangerous mission in itself with the rough seas) and got the crew to safety on one of the other boats. The older couple had to abandon their brand new yacht they had just started their cruise with down to Mexico, and lost their home as well as their retirement plan.

185

Fortunate for them, they were insured, but their cruising plans came to an immediate halt and the items they could rescue from their home in the weeks to follow were distributed amongst the other boats which helped in the rescue.   There is a safe anchorage on the other side of the island, but fortunate for us, we had very light winds anyway and are always mindful of the power of the weather.

We explored the island the next day, hoping to find a path to the top of the volcano, so I could look down the crater! We found a trail which took us half way round the island to the other side, and the light-house, but never did find a path to the top. It was a hot day and the island is covered in different species of cactus. Without a path, navigating was impossible; we were already being spiked by the hitch-hiking plants! The day was breathtaking, the scenery inconceivable, the plants astounding and the seals in the inland lagoon mischievous, we decided we didn't need to look down a crater anyway!

Diary excerpt 8th January 2004

We had difficulty finding paths amongst the curious ground scrub of diverse species of cactus, spiky bush and large grey ice plants. The most remarkable thing was lichen which was growing all over the cactus giving a really ghostly appearance to the lava-strewn landscape. The lava was jagged and razor-sharp and rounded near the shore where the water smoothed it off. One particular type of cactus attached itself to you with very sharp and protracted quills. If you got one on your trouser or shoe it was impossible to pick it off since it embedded it's spine into your clothing, even leather! We didn't find the top unfortunately since the scrub got too dense and the lava flow had formed sharp ridges impossible to walk along, so we satisfied ourselves by walking a good half way around the island before heading back the same way. We visited the 'wreck' on the beach but didn't stick around for long once we spotted an armed guard who we assumed was supervising the salvage of the vessel.

Next we are heading for Isla Cedros which is a night sail and a full day, where we will stop for an overnight rest before a day-hop to Turtle Bay (which will then be about halfway to La Paz). The weather is definitely getting warmer and the scenery really different. The back drop of the towering mountains are crimson and jagged, like the pictures you see of Arizona, and a chain of volcanoes lie along the coastline, some of which you can clearly see the craters. Sand dunes, porpoise, sea lions and plenty of whale spotting makes the day-sail a lot more appealing, especially when you can sit outside in the sun!

Approaching Isla Cedros, the author reads a book on deck.

Isla Cedros was incredible. The North anchorage was alive with wild-life, colossal elephant seals were feeding their new born pups (who squealed like chimps), Pelicans and different types of sea birds swooped and fed from the little schools of fish and playful harbour seals jumped and played around the boat. We had 60ft visibility in crystal clear water and the mountains towered over us, alight in the sunshine and looking very majestic with their steep clefts and arroyos. I wish we could have anchored here, but we were concerned if the wind kicked up from the north, so moved further south to a more protected anchorage.

Diary excerpt 9th January 2004

Cedros Island is a completely marvellous island, just magnificent! Peaked mountains carved into yawning canyons with colonies of gigantic elephant seals that have just birthed. You can watch the babies suckling the massive mothers who use their flippers to flap sand over the babies to keep them cool. The baby elephant seals sound like chimpanzees and the adults have a high pitched bark. The young harbour seals leap and bound around the boat in schools of 20 or 30, tumbling over each other and then excitedly somersaulting and jumping high out of the water. These excitable youngsters are really inquisitive and take delight in racing the boat as we were leaving the bay. The water visibility is crystal clear down to depths of 60 feet so you can plainly see their antics underwater from the deck of the boat.

The mountains look desolate until we spied through the binoculars an enormous cactus growing abruptly up the hillside, the great grey ice cactus has a hefty flower head growing out the top, blossoming vivid lime green and yellow flora. At the right time of year this mountain side must be a riot of colour with the entire cactus in bloom. This IS paradise, the amalgamation of dramatic mountains, crystal blue waters and nature so loud and prolific you hardly know where to look next! Against a blue azure sky and a bright sun, it really couldn't be any more perfect or beautiful, a truly spectacular place!

Turtle Bay was our next stop after pulling the anchor at 2 a.m. and heading out. The seas were a bit rolly, but we arrived at the anchorage early afternoon. This is a large sheltered bay with a fascinating, if a little disheartened town, but with basic supplies and an internet cafe!!!! The internet is slow and expensive at $5 an hour, and the @ key does not work, so the first time I tried to email it was unsuccessful, however, it was nice to be back in touch again with our friends and family since this was our only means of communication. The people were very gracious and we felt very ignorant not being able to communicate very efficiently with them in Spanish. They were amused by our attempts though and very smiley and accommodating. This town is very cut-off from the rest of Baja and has only one road which is in very bad repair, making supplies few and far between.

We had one very amusing episode when Greg was trying to find out if there were any 'wash rooms' nearby. He proudly read from his Spanish book.

"Donde Este la Caballero?"

The Mexican gent looked at Greg as though he was a little crazy, so Greg shouted it a bit louder and pointed to his zipper. This seemed to get an even crazier response until we tried another word which he comprehended. We later found out that he was asking "Where are the men?" as he was pointing at his zipper, which was probably why they responded the way they did!

We decided to stay there and get a few jobs done and explore. We climbed to the top of one of the mountains and was rewarded with an extraordinary view of a desert landscape framed by sheer pointed mountains of diverse rusty red, orange and sand, and again, different types of cactus. The outlook from the summit of the mountain on one side showed the whole bay, the yachts at anchor looking like little black dots. The contrary view to the bay was an infinite desolate desert. The mountain in the distance was about 30 miles away so that gives you some idea how good the visibility was that day! The desert road which would lead to Morro Santo Domingo and the bay was the only road into Turtle Bay and you could clearly see the rough scar across the desert

The weather was great, mostly in the 25-30C range and not dropping at night below 16C...which was fantastic!!! The beach which led to the desert landscape was really striking, although the surf was a bit tricky to navigate and land the dinghy! We managed to land the dinghy in the surf without mishap, but we weren't so lucky when we headed back to the boat. As we timed the waves to push off the dinghy a rogue wave broke over the bow of the boat, filling the dinghy with water and giving us both a thorough soaking. We were saturated by the time we got back to the boat, the cold wind causing us to shiver in our wet clothes, but it was well worth it. It was good to walk behind the beach through the desert landscape we had spotted from the peak of the mountain.

The locals were really entrepreneurial and used their fishing pangas to come out to the boat and offer any services they could. Their wives offered a laundry service (which most boats took advantage of since they had a lack of fresh water), and the men organised diesel or gas delivery. We took advantage of the laundry and diesel delivery and even allowed them to dispose of our garbage. We did hear that their way of disposing the garbage was to sort through it in their boat to find anything useful and then throw the rest overboard! For many of the yachties this was an appalling sight since we had been carrying around the garbage bags for proper disposal for days and sometimes weeks!

Many of the boats were very generous with their 'tips' giving much needed clothes or school supplies for the children, and the locals always looked forward to the arrival of yachts for these reasons.

The Miniature 'village'

As we sailed into the Bay we spotted minuscule multi-coloured houses away from the main town and couldn't work out through the binoculars what they were, so we decided to investigate. We hiked for an hour into the mountains and valleys behind the main town, following a well trod path, to the settlement of miniature houses painted in dazzling pinks, greens, pastel blues and yellows and decorated with many plastic flowers. Each petite house was complete with glass windows and a diminutive locked door and we spotted through the windows a small alter with photographs and memorabilia of their dead. We couldn't help but notice that the dead were living better than some of the residents in the main town who didn't always have glass windows or doors on their homes. Looking close-up to one of the funeral homes demonstrated how neat and tidy this area is kept, although they throw the garbage just over the fence which marks the area. We looked inside one of the funeral homes and saw all the toys and belongings of this child who had an early death. It was so sad to see but we felt awed by the level of respect they pay their dead too. We gathered that some funeral houses had several family members and dated back as far as the 1960's so these buildings are obviously maintained frequently because they looked so clean and neat. This is so contradictory to their homes which are dust strewn with rubbish everywhere that it seemed a travesty that they treated their dead better than the living.

Diary excerpt 18th January

After 8 days in Turtle Bay and exploring the village, we set off south again. It turned out to be a wonderful passage, variable wind and a 6-7 foot swell from the North West which gave us a nice downwind sail. We spotted 3 whales which we watched for about an hour, sounding and diving and they came quite close at one point. As the wind picked up from the North West we

190

approached Asuncion Island and our anchorage for the night off the village.

We didn't go ashore that night but made the best of a good weather window and headed for Aberojos at first light. Greg tried to fish again and ended up losing the whole rig, weight, line and sinker, so we need to ask around about getting the right gear! We've spent so much on fishing licenses it would be nice to re-coup some of that cost on edible fish! We're both looking forward to getting to Magdalena Bay and having another rest.

The panorama on the coastline is really glorious, the mountains are diverse vibrant colours and the ranges are different heights and shapes giving an interesting view as we slowly sail pass them.

Bahia Santa Maria

We stopped first at Bahia Santa Maria which is the 'outside' bay to Magdalena Bay since we had been told it was really beautiful, and it was an incredibly stunning anchorage. We anchored first close to the mountains and off a small beach where we had access to a low valley across the mountains to the other side. We had a fantastic day walking through the valley, spotting many gorgeous wild flowers and different varieties of cacti (we are still fascinated by cacti - especially the flowering ones). The walk was so absorbing with lots of different rock formations and types of rock to gaze at, many different plants and even the occasional hare (yes, we frightened a poor thing and it hopped away!) We saw plenty of other animal tracks and heard coyote.

The walk to the other side was hot, but we were rewarded by a spectacular view across the Pacific Ocean and along to the lighthouse on the Cape. The following day we moved the boat to a different anchorage, near the sand dunes, and were left quite alone when the other two boats keeping us company departed. We skinny-dipped in the water, which was cool, but refreshing in the hot sun. We then decided to walk the beach in search of sand dollars and shells, and investigate the sand dunes.

We started a leisurely walk along the beach and before we knew it, had started to meander into the dunes. We spotted a high dune in the distance and decided to scale to the top...we didn't realize at the time, it was actually on the other side (i.e. the Magdalena Bay side). We had an extraordinary day walking amongst 20ft sand dunes and were quite exhausted by the time we reached the highest dune. The view was unbelievable...looking over a 5 mile range of 20ft dunes one side, and the mangrove estuary of Magdalena Bay on the other. By the time we got back to the boat, we had clocked up around 10 miles and a healthy looking tan!

Standing on the pinnacle of the highest sand dune looking back over 5 miles of 20 feet dunes we'd walked through to get there.

One of the many wild cactus that fascinated the author

Magdalena Bay and shops with no produce

We moved to Magdalena Bay, which we walked to the previous day across the sand dunes, but by sea it took us 7 hours to sail!!! In a way, I wish we had spent more time at Bahia Santa Maria, it had a much wilder unspoilt beauty about it and we were quite alone. Magdalena Bay is also quite attractive, but not the same.

We anchored for the first week off the village, waiting for fresh supplies and the dream of fresh barbecued chicken and cold beer. The supplies in the village were very limited with 2 or 3 Tienda's (basically one room at the front of their home) which sold a few tin goods and fresh vegetables and meat only on the day of delivery. There was no ice or refrigeration so nothing kept in the heat longer than a few days. Every day we visited to find out when the Panga was due with supplies and every day the fishing Panga's buzzed us as they passed close to our boat. The curious fisherman got great satisfaction passing close to the boat; they particularly enjoy doing this at 5 a.m. when they set off for their morning fishing expeditions!

We did have some very enjoyable walks across the mountains behind the village and our curious eyes had plenty to keep us busy as we watched the villagers whilst drinking our morning coffee. We decided to leave for the quieter anchorage off the sand dunes and later found out that that was the day the delivery arrived!

The Port captain happily visited our boat for the paper work and port fees, climbing onboard in his cut-off white Wellingtons and immediately inviting himself down below so that he can check out what we might have to give him. Of course we had no beer and we'd depleted our supplies of other alcohol, so we could only offer coffee and biscuits. He gladly accepted but kept asking for beer or whiskey (which I think other boats gladly give him). The fact that we had limited conversation with our poor Spanish and his Basic English worked in our favour for a change. Paying port fees could have been avoided if we had just stayed in the Paradise of Santa Maria - oh well, that is hindsight for you!

The anchorage off the dunes was much quieter and much more picturesque. The dunes are pure white and quite striking. We spent many hours walking the beach and collecting the many different types of shells. The sand spit that extended out from the west side of the sand dune anchorage was always inhabited by hundreds of Pelicans, Curlews and other sea birds and they let me walk pretty close to them before they decided to fly away. (This is where the photograph on the front cover was taken).

There was an 'eco camp' onshore set up for the tourists who come to whale watch and their occupants always provided good entertainment through the binoculars! We walked across the sand dunes to Bahia Santa Maria and looked across the bay to where we were anchored last week.

The Mangrove Forest

 There is a mangrove forest which can be accessed at high tide and you can ride your dinghy right through the mangroves and spot many amazing birds. We spent a few hours exploring the inland waters of the mangroves in the company of another dinghy from the Yacht Exodus, and took the waterways as far into the mangroves that we could get our inflatable. It is a really scenic mangrove forest, clean and healthy with lots of new growth and plenty of wildlife. Since this is the first anchorage that has given us almost constant sunshine and beautiful surroundings, we're not in a rush to leave! Although other cruisers have spotted many whales in 'Magdalena' Bay, it seems most of the sightings are in the entrance, and so, on our last day, we anchored for the evening off the small fishing camp, and indeed, saw many. We also heard another yacht on the radio talking about his anchorage called Soledad, at the north end of 'Magdalena' Bay, in the estuary, where he was watching the whales nurse right next to his boat.

Passage to Cabo San Lucas

We set off for the last overnight passage to Cabo and as we arrived off Cabo Falso the sun rose and we were rewarded with magnificent sightings of whales doing full breaches close by the boat. This was the largest sighting of whales we had seen and we took much delight in watching them as we admired the architecture of the condos and hotels that lined the beachfront. There are many multi-million dollar buildings, brilliantly painted in coral, orange, yellow and reds, and balanced on the rock faces, nestled next to impressive hotels and providing a multi-coloured splash of arches and windows facing out to sea. As we rounded Cabo the magnificent natural rock 'arches' came into sight, gleaming white in the morning sunshine, very imposing!!! The famous arches of Cabo framed an old square rigger in the distance on a whale tour and made for a very photogenic moment. This anchorage lived up to it's rolly reputation (even in very calm weather which we had) so we opted to stay on the boat and just rest for the night before leaving for Los Frailes the following morning. We did visit the Cabo Yacht club to take on fresh water and diesel, and learnt that the mooring fees were over $100 per night!

The author using Seafire's cockpit to categorize the many shells collected at the beach, Bahia Santa Maria, Baja California, Mexico

Los Frailes

Our sail to Los Frailes started off pretty smoothly, motoring north through 3-4ft sharp wind waves, but with little wind. Within a few hours of reaching the anchorage the wind had picked up to 15-20kts on the nose and the waves hitting us on the beam....uncomfortable for a few hours, but otherwise an

195

uneventful passage. The anchorage has a really stunning setting; it can only be described as paradise, with perfect white sand beaches and aquamarine waters. We spent a week and half in this paradise, hiking through the cactus landscape, exploring the mountains, scrambling to the top for the best views, and snorkelling in the clear chilly water!!! We followed the dusty road into the wilderness and really enjoyed clambering amongst the giant cactus. I commented that the rock formations were so clean and bright that they looked like a desert theme park made of Styrofoam! The dusty road that led to the beach made for interesting and easy hiking with only the odd Recreational vehicle coming or going. You could see the sandy cutting through the wilderness and if you wanted you could walk all the way to Cabo Pulmo to the North, which would be the nearest town for supplies. However, we found the cactus so interesting that every time we set off to do that, we lost track of time and grew hot and tired pretty quickly.

The R.V. community there was really friendly and invited us to join in their various activities and share their stories. We were really impressed by some of the gardens and clay ovens they had built for their winter retreat. This area was a secret paradise shared only with a few, so it was not the kind of place a casual traveller would even find. Many of the 'Snowbirds' were Canadian and had all passed through many of the same 'ports' that we had called in on down the USA coast (even some remembered seeing us in Coos Bay)

Los Frailes, Baja California, Mexico - giant cactus

The Provision truck

Several times a week, various government supply trucks visited the area to provide much needed provisions for the local fishing village, and the R.V.'s and yachts also took their turn to buy everything from chicken to fresh vegetables and fruit at subsidised prices. The local villagers lived side by side in harmony with the Snowbirds (tourist who travel south for the winter) and sold fresh fish to them, developing close relationships with the women in the camp and helping to supply clothes and school supplies to the children. The atmosphere of the area was one of strong social bonding between the Americans, Canadians and Mexicans and of mutual respect.

Priority was always given to the Mexicans when the provision trucks arrived, the Snowbirds patiently waiting in line whilst the Mexicans crowded around the truck to get first pick. The trucks would take special requests from the Snowbirds so you could 'order' anything special you wanted, and they didn't inflate the prices, charging 'gringo' prices as some of the larger tourist towns are inclined to do! We were soon barbecuing that chicken we've been waiting for since leaving San Diego (In fact our first fresh meat since leaving there!)

We could even hike to a small hotel at the opposite end of the beach that would sell you ice cold beers at very reasonable prices. We would really enjoy the 30 minute hike along the beach and a short way through the mountains with the reward of an ice cold beer at the end. Greg would pack the beers into his backpack and fit in as much crushed ice around them to keep them cold. By the time we reached the boat his back would be frozen cold with the melted ice and soaking wet, but we still had icy cold beers at the end.

Some days the anchorage proved to be fairly windy, perfectly safe, but a wet dinghy ride and landing on the beach. As soon as the winds and waves died down, we set off for our final leg to La Paz, anchoring overnight in Muertos to split up the bash north into the Sea of Cortez.

The following morning we had a fantastic smooth sea and light winds, Isla Cerralvo blocking the old North wind waves from the sea, and providing a flat passage to La Paz.
Diary excerpt 19th February 2004

At last!!!!! Nearly 6 months and 2263 sea miles since leaving Nanaimo, we arrived in Bahia Lobos on the 19th February 2004, where we spent a wonderful afternoon and evening, before approaching the 'Santa Cruz' virtual marina, the following morning. Little did we know, Carnival had just started, so we spent the first 5 days here, listening to live music, eating fabulous junk food and watching the colourful parades! Since then we've been taking advantage of all the facilities a great city has to offer and sorting out paper work etc... In the next few weeks our adventure will continue as we cruise the 29 islands of the Sea of Cortez.

The 'Santa Cruz' virtual marina was an anchorage area with moorings for $77 a month, giving you use of hot showers and a dinghy dock. You had to pay a small daily fee for anchoring in La Paz harbour so it wasn't that much more expensive to pay for the 'virtual marina'. The view from the anchorage was of the 'Malecon' which was a 'Promenade' along the waterfront and always provided entertainment watching the coming and goings of the locals. Despite La Paz having an airport and decent paved road, it is not really a 'tourist' destination, so the only travellers you tended to see were 'backpackers' or independent travellers, so the Carnival was definitely a 'local' affair.

Mardi Gras in La Paz

The streets got really busy for Carnival with 95% of the crowd being local Mexicans and a handful of yachties and tourists. Every evening the floats of the parade would start their procession down the Malecon and the streets were 6 or 7 people deep. Each float was vibrant and extravagant, no expense was spared on the elaborate costumes of the princesses and the music was loud and passionate. Various themes were adopted by various clubs and organisations, the local beer companies the most popular with eye-catching 'Tecate' girls dressed in skimpy red and white corporate costumes and in competition with the 'Pacifico' girls in stretch Lycra electric blue skimpy shorts. The procession took

198

place for 5 days and by the 5th day the princesses were sporting slightly dirty and torn gowns and the props had evidence of daily repairs. The beer was flowing and the bands loud and entertaining. Street food was prolific and the special 'hamburgesa' stand provided carnival entertainment when the Mexican cook danced with his various condiment bottles dressing the burgers.

Mexicans love the opportunity to party and they are real night owls, dancing until 2 or 3 am in the morning and shopping until they drop, buying the most unexpected items such as thick woolly blankets and plates. In fact, we found the 'blanket' stands one of the most entertaining, with commentators shouting into cheap microphones to attract the customers, piling the blankets high and throwing in extras to give incentives to the customers. The kitchenware stalls did the same, piling plates and dinner services until the customers couldn't physically carry the bargains they had bought. But carry them they did. Everywhere in the crowds we spotted Mexican fathers, following their wives and children, balancing piles of blankets and kitchenware as they struggled through the crowds, not allowing the burden to spoil their fun or cut their night short!

There was never any sign of violence or drunken bad behaviour as you would see in North America or England at such a public event where beer was consumed in volume in the street. Everyone was there to have a good time and celebrate the Carnival, and that's exactly what they did! After Carnival finished the streets were cleaned and the town looked like all those people had never been there.

Life returned to normal and we took advantage of the many large stores just out of town, which you could get to on local buses. We visited the multiplex cinema and caught up on the latest movies and ate wonderful hand made ice cream, fish tacos, and burritos. Eventually it was time to move on once we caught up with Bob and Rita on the Yacht Farewell and Bob and Doreen on the Yacht Scottish Mist. We were long enough in La Paz to give them both the opportunity to catch up with us. Our reunion with Bob and Doreen meant we could keep our promise to cruise some of the islands together.

Espiritu Santos

By early April we were ready to move on and explore the islands. We took our time, slowly motoring up the whole west coast of Espiritu Santos, nudging into each bay to check out the anchorages for future reference. The scenery was spectacular, with dramatic pink rock prevailing along the coastline. Some of the rock formations were an inconceivable colour and shape, the contours smooth and rounded by the waves and wind. We arrived in Partida Cove and immediately started to explore the island, which proved to have some magnificent hikes to several great vistas. The two islands of Partida Cove have a beach which forms a sand spit and joins the two islands. Access to this sand spit and the North Bay was dependant on the tides with very shoal water giving limited access in the dinghy. Care must be taken with the tides before approaching the beach because it is very shallow and you can end up walking your dinghy in soft mud for quite a distance!

On one occasion we came back from a hike to find our dinghy high and dry on the mud flats with the water dried out for miles (or so it seemed). We had to wade through the thick grey mud, sometimes up to our knees, being sucked into the sticky goo if you hesitated in your steps, a pretty horrid sensation. Bob and Doreen of Scottish Mist joined us on a strenuous hike and we all admired the view from a high point off the North beach. The hike took you through the arroyo and up as far as you could go and gave a fantastic view of the bay. We spotted many lizards of all sizes and admired the many giant cacti.

Unfortunately we were 'blown' out of this anchorage by a 30 knot westerly wind, making it a very uncomfortable ride. The swell started to roll across the bow of the boat, rising the front of the boat five feet into the air and then pitching violently as it smashed down into the next swell. This becomes a very uncomfortable motion inside the boat so we decided to move to a calmer anchorage.

San Evaristo

We sailed across to San Evaristo on the Baja side which was a delightful fishing village and the first place where you could buy very basic supplies, but we only bought fish from the local fisherman. The road leading to La Paz from here is little more than a donkey trail, and indeed we saw plenty of donkeys doing exactly that and captured some really special photos. Not only did the road lead to La Paz, it also led to remote villages in the mountains. The locals still used donkeys to transport water and other supplies from village to village and it was quite rare to see a vehicle on the road. We passed a Mexican on his donkey carrying water jugs whilst we walked on the road, and he greeted us with a friendly smile and wave.

This delightful fishing village had two bays, one to the south, and one to the North, both of which you could anchor in to suit different winds. We walked from one side to the other across beautiful desert mountains giving fantastic views. The view of the North anchorage was backed by massive salt drying flats, and this supplied the other source of income for these villagers. There seemed to be a plentiful supply of fresh water and the houses were all nestled in the shade of palms. We followed the 'road' to La Paz for a few miles and came across a deep arroyo which led to another village, and we assumed a ranch. A herd of cows from the ranch were taking shade in the arroyo under a small oasis of trees, but we couldn't see how far the ranch would be to walk too, so we turned around and headed back to the beach to cool down.

Isla San Francisco

Continuing our 'zig zag' sail up the sea of Cortez, we crossed to the stunning island of San Francisco. This incredibly breathtaking island had everything to offer with aquamarine water, a beautiful white sand beach and fascinating hikes with stunning views. A trail led across the top of the mountains to a panorama of the Sea of Cortez to the left and the perfect semi-circular bay and beach to the right.

By the 4th day the anchorage was beginning to get busy, so we had a beach party to meet everyone on the other yachts. Each boat brought a dish to share and one motor yacht arrived with a giant tub of ice cream! Who could wish for anything more perfect than ice cream in paradise? It goes without saying all these remote islands have no stores! We really enjoyed this anchorage and would have certainly stayed longer if the wind had not switched to the South West, which created a 5ft fetch into our

North West anchorage. Once again we woke at 5.00 a.m. as the boat pitched in the swell, just like it did in Partida. It appeared that the boats tucked into the hook were sheltered from the swell, so it was a shame there was no more room!

Julie pearched on the high trail looking down at the perfect beach at Isla San Francisco, Baja California, Mexico.
The dot in the ocean is Yacht Seafire at anchor.

Los Gatos

As soon as the sun rose we pulled anchor and headed back to Evaristo for a protected anchorage, leaving the next day for Los Gatos on the Baja side. This anchorage has the most unbelievable geology and we had an incredible week exploring the vibrant sandy pink mountains and rock picking the many geodes.

Each day we hiked a different area, returning with arms full of extraordinary rocks and shells. The south anchorage was tucked between two reefs and gave easy access to the beach which had a multi-coloured rock face made up of many different shapes and colours of rocks with many geodes. Some of the rocks we collected had crystals at different stages and some were well-formed perfect crystals. Once we knew what to look for we also found many on the beach which had been broken free by rock falls, and we spent many engaging hours breaking open the red rocks to reveal the geodes. The north anchorage (which we moved to when the wind changed) gave access to the smooth coral coloured rocks sitting on a pink sand beach. These were fun to explore, finding fascinating shapes formed by the wind and waves, such as women's legs and shapely bottoms. You could climb the undulating red domes creating remarkable stepping stones and enthralling views.

Aqua Verde

We had heard so many good reports of this place, and they were all completely true. The south anchorage was a true paradise with aqua clear waters like a swimming pool and a really interesting village with a fantastic Tienda selling great fresh vegetables and meat. The villagers were farmers and many goats and cows wandered the mountains alone leaving plenty of trails to follow. We also spent some time in the North anchorage, which also had the clear waters, but not as beautiful as the south anchorage. We opted to stay a little longer so I could spend my birthday there, and I can honestly say, I can't think of a more wonderful place to celebrate. Early in the day of my birthday (around 5.30 am) we heard drums and music right outside the boat and rushed on deck to find Doreen and Bob all dressed up with Mardi Gras beads and headdresses, banging saucepans with wooden spoons and singing 'Happy Birthday'. The previous day Doreen had asked me what I would like for my birthday, and I had 'joked' a 'full English breakfast with sausage, eggs and bacon and fresh baked bread!' Doreen, somehow pulled this off, and together with the music and costumes she had delivered a full English breakfast for the 4 of us, kept warm in a large serving plate with a lid. They climbed aboard and we had a birthday breakfast complete with Birthday cake and candles! One of the most memorable birthdays and one of the best presents I ever received! Their boat had a compact freezer and full fridge, whereas we had neither, so they were able to use their limited supplies to provide this treat! It is amazing how you miss the small 'luxuries' in life!

Aqua Verde anchorage

Honeymoon Cove, Isla Dizante, Baja California, the author could paddle ashore to the private beach from the anchorage.

Honeymoon Cove, Isla Dizante

Another favourite, this stunning island looked dramatic as we approached it, with its many peaks and arroyos giving the impression of large folds of silk reflected in the sun. The tiny north bight anchorage was just big enough for our boat, stern anchored. We could plainly see the reef on each side of the boat and the clear water highlighted the many multi-coloured fish which swam around the boat. We could see how this anchorage was christened 'Honeymoon' cove being so remote and private. The snorkelling here was great and we saw countless varieties of starfish with diverse colours and designs. They were some of the brightest ones I'd ever seen, so we couldn't resist lifting them out the water for a quick photograph before we returned them to their homes.

Diary excerpt 24th April

We anchored forward and stern off the beach, and snuggled into the tiny north bight anchorage in crystal clear water surrounded by tropical fish, it was like being anchored in an aquarium! We had our own 'mini' private beach which was really picturesque and had lots of trails leading off it, giving unbelievable views and photo opportunities. The water was warm and the snorkelling was great; lots of different kinds of tropical fish, big schools of damsel and zebra fish, who we could feed bread to from the cockpit of the boat. We counted 7 different kinds of fish just swimming around the boat. This is the most stunning anchorage, definitely no need to get off the boat here! You can be entertained just sitting in the cockpit watching all the fish swim around.

Isla Carmen, Puerto Ballandra

This was our favourite area for snorkelling where the rocks formed narrow canyons under the water and the fish sheltered from the sun. The snorkelling was really interesting here with great visibility and warm water with plenty to see. Apart from the many different species of multi-coloured fish, we spotted octopus and moray eels. The shoreline had interesting rock sculptures and arches, as well as nursery tide pools where you could spot the new-born fish. As we walked along the shoreline exploring we came across many seagulls nesting and almost stumbled across a Seagull on a nest with a baby seagull that looked like it had not long been born. The nest was so accessible we didn't realise we were walking amongst their nesting area and made a hasty retreat as soon as the seagulls started to squawk and dive-bomb us! A trail led to the other side of the island but we were prevented from investigating too far by the countless insects and the heat. It was very lush and had many green trees and flowering bushes and the golden grasses were simply beautiful, the flowering yellow bushes alive with the song of the honey bee.

Bahia Juanico

We had a bit of a bumpy ride getting here and we were surprised how flat the anchorage was, giving protection from the southerly swell as well as the old north west swell which gave us the lumpy ride in. A winsome anchorage with a miniature abrupt island connected to the beach by a sand spit and on top of the steep cliff it had impractical cactus growing right out the top. The beach on the other side of the island was too shallow to anchor in, but the near side gave good protection for two boats between the two reefs. We were anchored here with Scottish Mist and although it seemed like we had enough room, when the wind started to blow over 25 knots we both put out a 2nd anchor for fear of dragging on the nearby reefs. It was this reef and its jagged rocks which gave the anchorage such good protection. The spiky pinnacles had giant bird of prey nest's balanced right on the top and we watched them feeding young ones through the binoculars from our cockpit. A cheeky diving bird was really attracted to our boat and stayed with us the whole time we were anchored there. He was such a good swimmer and we watched him catching fish.

A trail led, behind the beach, to a great vantage point where we took lots of photos. A shrine had been made in a sheltered area at the back of the beach by all the sailing yachts which had visited this anchorage and it had boats recorded as far back as 20 years. They were really interesting to read, some carved in stone and wood, some written on shells and even a shoe, and so we added our own name written on a shell mobile for future visitors to look at.

Yacht Seafire and Yacht Scottish Mist at anchor in Bahia Juanico

Bahia Concepcion

This was going to be our jumping off port to cross the sea of Cortez to the mainland side and San Carlos. We only spent a few days here before heading across with a good weather window, so we didn't explore into the bay as much as we would have liked. This is the first time in the Sea of Cortez that we saw seaweed, and this was a very pretty but prolific hardy type which had the strength and appearance of plastic. You could just see it under the water and it was fun to row through watching the little fish that live amongst it. We were in search of the hot water spring, but just found a shady cave instead where fisherman probably stopped for a rest.

The houses nestled in the hills had really interesting architecture and almost blended into the mountain side with the natural stone clad walls. We knew we were back in civilization as soon as we saw these and the highway that runs alongside with the noisy trucks and their air breaks blasting across the bay. Up until now we had experienced nothing other than a few Mexican fishermen, a few Mexican farmers and basic Tiendas, lots of unspoilt nature and no roads or Motor Vehicles. It almost seemed like this road marked the end of our cruising. With the road came houses, tourists, loud trucks, buses and cars, bars and hotels. We often commented how unique the Baja is with the mountainous territory restricting access to anything other than boats for much of the coastal area.

This village was very pretty and the 'American' homes were nestled together with open fronts facing out to the beach. There were more houses behind the beach, where there was also a natural hot spring bath set in the village square. We enjoyed walking the village and made our way to the far end of the beach where we spotted a camp and bar. Here we met 'Michael' who was looking for a yacht who needed crew across to San Carlos. Although we had never taken crew before, we decided it would make the night passage an easier one with the extra hand and invited him along.

At night time the bay was alive with cat fish and a giant heron decided to use our dinghy as a diving platform to catch them. We watched from the cockpit as he carefully waited for the right moment and then snagged a big fish for his dinner! The following day the weather forecast was perfect, the moon was full and our extra crew member was ready to make the passage across the sea of Cortez to San Carlos.

This marked the end of our current voyage and a time to reflect on my travels in the last seven years. Not only had we run out of money several months ago, we already owed a decent amount on the credit card. The credit card would buy our tickets to England so I could find work, introduce Greg to the family and plan our next move.

Returning to England

We had been discussing our future and we had decided to extend our visit to the islands as long as possible before putting the boat in storage and flying to England. I was ready to face my family and friends again and I was looking forward to the challenge of work. I had not had a 'proper' job for seven years but I was confident my skills would enable me to start with senior office work as a temporary while I tried to get other employment. We didn't know how easy it would be to extend Greg's visa to stay there longer than the six months permitted, but we figured we would work that out when we got there! I knew the English pound was going to give us the best opportunity to quickly save enough money to continue our travels and we knew the boat would be very safe in storage in San Carlos. My parents were happy to give us accommodation in my family home for as long as we needed, so we knew we could keep our living expenses to a minimum.

We spent the next few weeks getting the boat ready for storage and packing our bags ready to live the next part of our life in England. I didn't realise at the time, but this journey marked the final leg of my circumnavigation of the globe. I hadn't really planned it this way, but quite by accident I had been travelling around the world, continuously in one direction, crossing every meridian, for the last seven years. Flying to England completed another circle, this time, all the way around the world.

We both suspected we wouldn't end up staying there too long, and indeed six months later we were using our return tickets to fly back to Mexico and our beloved Seafire. I managed to secure a 3 month marketing contract which gave me a great income, but Greg could not get an extension on his visa to stay in the U.K. so we decided to leave. I had spent enough years compromising my love and life for work so I wasn't about to make the same mistake again. The bonus from a very successful marketing campaign for a land investment company and salary I had made in 6 months was enough to pay off all our debts. I also negotiated a continued research project for the company while we lived on the boat in Mexico. We had managed to find a way of life which only cost an average of $800 a month and this meant we could continue this lifestyle for at least another 12 months living off 6 months salary. When the money ran out, we'd make a new plan then.

So how can you travel around the world for seven years on virtually no income?

Not everyone can live this way of life, most people require security, and can not adapt to a different lifestyle where modern appliances barely exist and the support network of extended family and friends is virtually non-existent. The ability to cope with the unknown, whether it is new places, languages, food or customs or overcoming the fear of battling storms and being alone in a vast ocean are not skills you can learn in an institution.

There is really no way before you try it to know if you can live with your partner in isolated confined quarters virtually 24 hours a day and 7 days a week. Many people think of this as an exotic life but many are easily bored if their minds are not constantly challenged and active or distracted by television, radio or newspapers. Perhaps the true definition of adventure is when the extraordinary becomes routine.

For me, the routine task of everyday life in the first world is a more difficult lifestyle. Carried back to a world where time is measured by something other than the sun, I didn't know how difficult it was going to be to become an ordinary citizen in the UK again. Dealing with the banks or immigration, insurance and household utilities seemed frustrating and complicated compared to the straightforward third world where you are responsible for your own water and power or refuse disposal.

Worrying about paying the rent or bills, owning the latest car or stereo equipment and wearing the latest fashion to meet the expectations of your job, is a constant challenge. Seven years away from the mainstream of life, experiencing diverse cultures, scenery and wildlife makes adjusting to a regular lifestyle and routine the real challenge. So much had changed in seven years and many things people just took for granted now were still unfamiliar to me, cell phones no longer looked like large radio transmitters, you could do something called 'text messaging' and you could access the internet from the public phone booths in England. Technology had left me behind and I was faced with gadgets that scanned your card at the supermarket and in the gas station and some cars didn't even require gas now! It made navigating the oceans, travelling alone across Lao and Cambodia and being at sea for 35 days easy by comparison.

I first thought I would not be able to fit back into the work environment, but as soon as I stopped looking for work as an "employee" I discovered my unique creative talent in marketing was actually easier to sell. I was given the opportunity by Peter Sage, Entrepreneur, to really shine. I was so passionate about life he could see that my potential was limitless. He made me realise that if you worked with passion the results could be incredible. I could achieve anything in my life and the work environment that I chose too. I made lots of money as a consultant, for him and for me, and once again I was playing the role of an Executive in the UK, but this time, one with a purpose (at that time to make enough money to sustain another year in Mexico).

Many people seem to admire my lifestyle and the things I have seen and done, but travelling around the world for seven years is not for everyone. Understanding what your passion in life really is and introducing that into your life is the first step. You can speed up this process with personal development workshops and retreats and reading inspirational books. You can start to live a more authentic life based on following your intuition and your heart and only making integrity based decisions. Do the things you love and that bring you joy because these are things you will be naturally the best at. Start to live life with more passion and purpose!

"The minute you begin to do what you really want to do, it's really a different kind of life" Buckminster Fuller

"There are two choices. You can make a living or you can design a life" Jim Ruhn

"Seek and you will find. Don't be willing to accept an ordinary life" Salle Merrill Redfield

AFTERWORD

My passion and purpose in life is to use my enthusiasm and joy to inspire and motivate others to live life with joy, happiness, laughter and fun and help one another to do the same.

I'm still in the process of designing that life now that I am settled in Victoria, B.C. with my beloved husband, Greg.

This is the 3rd edition of this book and since the first printing and the start of my business Distinctive Management Co. I have developed a programme of workshops and retreats to help other people "Find their passion in life" I have been featured on local TV and radio (Shaw Daily and CFAX1070AM) and I have established a loyal client base for my motivational coaching business. I am available for inspiring and motivational keynote speeches as well as local workshops and seminars.

I developed and launched a workbook and workshop package
"InspireABook"
" Be the author of your dreams"
In November 2007 to inspire and help first time authors to write and publish their own book. More information on the program can be found on my website www.inspireabook.com

Thank you for supporting LICADHO Canada and it's efforts in Cambodia by buying this book. More info at www.licadho.org For each book sold 5% of the profits will be donated to help disadvantaged girls and women in Cambodia.

I hope reading this book has inspired you to ask yourself what makes you really happy and take the first steps to changing your life to *live with passion and purpose!*

JULIE ANN SALISBURY

March 3rd 2008, Victoria, B.C. Canada.

QUICK ORDER FORM

All orders received by personal request will be signed by the author and can be requested the following ways:

By email: contact@nomadaroundtheworld.com

Telephone orders: 1-250-483-5791

See our website for more stories and photographs on www.nomadaroundtheworld.com/adventure

Postal orders: 104-3000 Stautw Rd, Saanichton, B.C. V8M 2K5

Please photocopy or tear off this page:

Name:

Address:

City/State/Province/Postal Code:

Tel:

Email:

Payment by Cheque, Money order or Paypal to Distinctive Management Co.

$19.95 US Dollars. $19.95 Can Dollars 9.95 UK Pound plus postage and packaging.

5% of all book sale profits will go towards disadvantaged girls and women in Cambodia.

ISBN 142517324-1